Resisting Apartheid America

RESISTING
APARTHEID AMERICA

Living the Badass Gospel

Miguel A. De La Torre

WILLIAM B. EERDMANS PUBLISHING COMPANY
GRAND RAPIDS, MICHIGAN

Wm. B. Eerdmans Publishing Co.
4035 Park East Court SE, Grand Rapids, Michigan 49546
www.eerdmans.com

Published 2023
Printed in the United States of America

29 28 27 26 25 24 23   1 2 3 4 5 6 7

ISBN 978-0-8028-8216-5

Library of Congress Cataloging-in-Publication Data

A catalog record for this book is available from the Library
of Congress.

DEDICATED TO

Senators
Ted Cruz (R-TX)
and
Marco Rubio (R-FL)

Contents

CONTENTS

Eurochristianity—America's Greatest Threat

We've all heard the myth. Persecuted English Separatist Puritans hazard an ocean voyage on the *Mayflower* seeking to worship God uninhibited from the religious persecutions of the Church of England and the Catholic Church. As pilgrims in a strange land, they established a foothold in the wilderness—the Plymouth Colony—for the glory of the one true God. But contrary to popular belief, this promised land which they supposedly tamed was never founded on the principle of freedom of religion, but rather on the principle of white supremacy. The concept of religious freedom was only applicable for white Anglo-Saxons. When these God-fearing pilgrims attacked the Pequot village in May 1637—putting women and children to the sword—the Puritan clergy, according to Captain John Underhill's journal, justified the massacre by casting the blame for the bloodbath on the alleged demonic beliefs of so-called Native savages.[1]

The role religion played for these first Euroamericans in establishing an enclave in this so-called new world was to provide spiritual justification for their ideology of white supremacy. Eurochristian nationalism is not a new phenomenon for our present age but has always been an ideal responsible for establishing the very foundation of an Anglo-Saxon nation. All who were not Anglo-Saxon simply were not welcome. Benjamin Franklin, the founding father who helped guide the Declaration of Independence, warned in 1751 of the need to prohibit those of "swarthy complexion" (he was referring to Germans) from migrating to Pennsylvania. He feared they were becoming "so numerous as to Germanize us instead of our Anglifying them."[2] By the early nineteenth century, it was the Irish who were not considered to be white, referred to as "n*ggers turned inside out," while those who were of African descent were commonly referred to as "smoked Irish."[3] By the start of the next century, it was the Italians' turn not to be white, commonly referred to as "white n*ggers."[4]

The nation which emerged from those original thirteen colonies was based on maintaining the purity of Anglo-Saxon whiteness. Those hailing from other white European countries were defined as not being white enough. They faced discrimination, abuse, violence, and even death. If white people can be so sadistic to other white people for not being white enough, what can those possessing too much melanin expect? In the established US hierarchy of race, Anglo-Saxons occupied the pinnacle, followed by those who had to learn how to become white—the Germans, the Irish, the Italians. The lesson learned is that whiteness, as a social construct, can be obtained if those once seen as not being white enough learn how to hate and oppress Others still considered nonwhite. Yes, whiteness can be learned; but there are those whose very appearance—specifically their Indigenous, Asian, or African features and skin pigmentation—prevents them from ever being able to make the transition to whiteness, regardless of how many generations they reside in this nation or how hard they attempt assimilation. They will perpetually be relegated—politically and spiritually—to the underside of whiteness.

Let's face it, America became a global empire whose humble roots were originally planted in the soil of white supremacy. This new republic has always been an apartheid nation, whose laws, customs, and traditions were constructed to ensure the power, privilege, and profit of whites—a government of whites, by whites, for whites. Those considered sacred were to remain separated from those consigned to the profane. Those who are not white can live in this America, but only as minoritized second-class citizens, or as the US Constitution would implicitly state for Blacks—three-fifths of a white person. For the first two hundred years of existence Euromales in America (many of whom were unqualified) were assured an affirmative action that ensured their possession of unearned status.

This apartheid structure began to show cracks in the 1970s. As civil rights legislation began to take hold, as white women began to demand equal rights, as the queer community demanded dignity, a socio-political power shift began. With the capture of the White House by a politically moderate Black man in 2008, it appeared the promise of equality might actually become a reality. But the inability of keeping the White House white scared white America. The desecration of this *White* House was simply a bridge too far to cross in the name of political correctness. For many Euroamericans, this was no longer the America in which they grew up. A cry arose in the land for a return to the America captured in television series like the 1960s CBS *Andy Griffith Show* about a sheriff in the mystical Southern town of Mayberry, North Carolina, where there were no Black people. Make America Great Again became the new "Battle Hymn of the Republic" to return to this nostalgic past where Blacks, and other people of color, were neither seen nor heard.

Even though Euromales, and token Eurowomen, still represented most of those occupying posts in government, business, and clergy, for a moment in time, until the election of "45," advances were being made to expand the promise of "liberty and justice for all." Unfortunately, we know all too well how the story ended. The response to a Black man

God! does everybody have the first same explanation for Trump?

Eurochristianity—America's Greatest Threat

leading a historically white supremacist nation resulted in a whitelash with the election of Donald Trump who rode a tidal wave of white fear and anger into the White House. Four years of white rage mattered. The little progress of expanding the rhetoric of American liberty that began to take root in the early 1970s was snuffed out. The political drama of the Trump years, and the collective post-traumatic stress that followed, accelerated a sectarian divide. America now finds itself on track toward reestablishing an apartheid system where the white minority continues to rule. If such a political and economic system cannot be legally reestablished, the alternative will likely be a violent tearing apart.

Sectarianism is usually a religious term used to describe friction between different faith traditions. Think of the European religious wars of the sixteenth, seventeenth, and eighteenth centuries between Catholics and Protestants, or the tensions existing between Sunnis and Shiites. Because Eurochristianity serves as the spiritual basis for the white supremacy of Euroamericans, the religious term *sectarianism* is apropos in understanding the political divisions forming against those who refuse to bow their knees to the white God. This new sectarianism is forming and solidifying within the United States pitting Eurochristianity against a pluralist democracy. White supremacy has historically dismissed people of color and their views, who tend to lean more liberal, as being inferior.

But Eurochristianity adds a new dimension to this historical precedent. Not only are those seeking to advance a more just society perceived as intellectually inferior, but they are also immoral, haters of America, enemies of the one true white God. What once was a difference of political positions resolved every two years at the polls has become a religious crusade against the immoral and inferior where winning, by any means possible—even through the employment of violence—becomes the will of the white God. Sectarianism becomes more than simply differing and disagreeing with another's faith or political view. A rooted hatred for the Other prevails, a hatred unto death. Defeating one's political opponent is not enough. There is a desire that they be humiliated and decimated.

Consider the photoshopped video posted by Congressman Paul Gosar (R-AZ) in 2021 on his official Twitter account depicting himself as a popular anime character decapitating Congresswoman Alexandria Ocasio-Cortez (D-NY) and swinging two swords at President Biden—a tweet cheered on by other Republican leaders and congressional members. Of course, he is not alone. Congresswoman Marjorie Taylor Greene (R-GA)—who asserted the 2021 California wildfires were ignited by space lasers controlled by Jewish bankers—was stripped of her committee assignments in early 2021 for endorsing violence against Democrats prior to her election. On her Facebook campaign page, she posted a photo of herself holding a gun alongside isolated images of Representatives Ocasio-Cortez, Ilhan Omar (D-MN), and Rashida Tlaib (D-MI) under the caption "Squad's worst nightmare." Representatives Gosar and Greene are but the tip of the iceberg. According to a study conducted by Reuters, almost eight hundred election officials in twelve states have received intimidating messages from Trump supporters during 2021 after claims of a stolen election were made,[5] while Congressional members experienced a 107 percent increase of threats in 2021 compared with 2020.[6]

Violence and the threat of violence against political liberals and people of color have been on the rise ever since Trump first ran for office in 2016. Remember his May 2016 response to a pair of Massachusetts men who urinated on the face of a homeless Latino they encountered before beating him with a metal pipe while yelling "Donald Trump is right. All these illegals need to be deported." Rather than denouncing the violence done in his name, he initially praised the passion demonstrated by his followers, commenting, "They love this country, they want this country to be great again." Only after mounting criticism did he condemn the violence days later.[7] This was a candidate who encouraged violence during his own campaign rallies, cheering devotees to "knock the hell" out of protesting hecklers.

Four years of Trump's toxic masculinity has normalized political violence, seen in its full manifestation on January 6th. Like religious sectarians of bygone centuries, today's Trump devotees find themselves engaged in a holy war seeking to preserve the purity of their sacred status within the promised land of a white America. The storming of the Capitol, as seen on our television sets, was not enough to dissuade this emerging sectarianism. Quite the contrary. Rather than abating, it has grown bolder, more commonplace. During a western Idaho conservative rally held by a local state representative in October 2021, a young man approached the microphone to ask when they could begin shooting Democrats. "When do we get to use the guns?" he inquired as the audience applauded. "How many elections are they going to steal before we kill these people?"[8] He is not alone in his sentiments. According to a poll taken after the January 6th insurrection, 30 percent of Republicans (11 percent of Democrats) believe "things have gotten so far off track, [that] true American patriots may have to resort to violence in order to save our country." More disturbing is that 26 percent of white evangelicals, 19 percent of white Catholics, and 17 percent of Protestants agree with this statement. Among Eurochristian nationalists, who believe "God has granted America a special role in human history," the acceptance of political violence hovers at 27 percent.[9] So much for following the Prince of Peace. The employment of violent speech and use of physical force by one of the two major political parties in the name of their white God is now seen as justifiable.

Euroamerican Republicans and Democrats may each see the other as the greatest existential threat to their well-being; but for those on the margins of whiteness, the threat to the well-being of people of color is both Euroamerican Republicans *and* Democrats. And while it is true that Republicans are rapidly becoming the party of white supremacism, that does not mean—in some neat dualistic fashion—that Democrats are the savior of people of color. They are just as racist. The issue faced by those on the margins is not between a good and a bad political party, but between a bad and a worse political party. During Jim and Jane Crow, the Democrats were the worse political party. During today's Trumpism, the Republicans are the worse political party. Who knows if in some near future their roles will flip again?

I just...

Biden may have run for office on the promise of bipartisanism—as did Obama and Bush before him—but unfortunately, there does not seem to be any desire to move away from the America envisioned by sectarian Trumpists. The mishandling of the coronavirus pandemic probably played a greater role in Trump losing reelection than his toxic masculinity. There were those who hoped that the election of Biden would be a repudiation of the Eurochristian nationalism advocated and defended by Trump. Such hope, however, was misplaced. True, Trump lost the 2020 reelection; but the white Eurochristian nationalism he and his minions represent was never repudiated. Biden may have garnered

9

some eight million more votes than Trump, but this does not mean he won by eight million more votes.

Biden's victory was in fact razor thin. Just consider that if Trump would have acquired 5,890 more votes in Georgia, 5,229 more votes in Arizona, and 10,342 more votes in Wisconsin, he would have secured a second term. The electoral vote would have been tied at 269 each, transferring the decision, according to the Constitution, to the House of Representatives elected that same Tuesday night. And while it would appear the Democrats had the advantage, being that they narrowly captured the House, voting does not occur based on each member being granted a single vote. Instead, state delegations vote as one, and thanks to gerrymandering, Republicans had the advantage on election night 2020. All this to say that Trump did not lose by eight million votes; he instead lost by 21,461 votes! We obviously do not live in a functioning democracy where each vote counts equally. This close division only demonstrates that the political mechanisms undergirding white supremacy put in place at the founding of the republic remain just as potent in 2020.

Regardless of four years of overt racism and sexism and heterosexism, four years of incompetent executive management, four years of advocating sectarian sentiments, and four years of articulating a flood of lies, most Euroamericans who claim Christian identity rejected the truth Jesus promised about being set free. More Eurochristians voted for Trump in 2020, after witnessing his anti-gospel words and actions played out on the national stage, than voted for him as a relatively unknown in 2016. A correlation exists between Euroamericans who attend a religious service at least once a month and support for Trump. Consider that during the 2020 election, 84 percent of white evangelicals, 57 percent of white Protestants, and 57 percent of white Catholics cast their votes for Donald Trump. Compare this to the 2016 election where the level of support among fewer voters was respectively 77 percent, 57 percent, and 64 percent.[10]

Eurochristianity and Trumpism are twins of white supremacy. Evangelicals were a fixture at the White House, laying hands on the President, praying for him to indeed make America Christian again. They cried out *Kaiser kurios*. The apostasy of offering devotion to a man by proclaiming "Caesar is Lord" was politically expedient because it gained them conservative seats on the Supreme Court bench committed to overturning *Roe*. These Euroamericans who voted for the antithesis of the gospel message obviously believe in a God. It just so happens that their God, created in their image, is as white as their Lord. This is a white God who blesses subverting the democratic process if it can maintain apartheid structures that protect and expand Eurochristianity.

For those dissatisfied with a liberal democracy that seeks a more just social and economic order, violence is spiritually justified in the name of populist demagogues whenever

What in the absolute Fuck?

political power cannot be legitimately won. Once Eurochristians are secured in positions of power, attacks are unleashed on the safeguards of democracy, specifically the free press, constitutional checks and balances, an independent judicial system, and respect for the loyal opposition. The very structures that ensure free and open elections are usurped through lies and false, unproven accusations of fraud. Political hacks are appointed whose loyalties are to the demagogue as opposed to the Constitution. Soon, democracy becomes an empty husk filled by authoritarian wannabes. This playbook has been employed by past and present dictatorial figures who were originally elected to political positions, only to undermine the very structures that brought them to power so they could rule unopposed. Think of figures on the right like Germany's Hitler and Hungary's Orbán or on the left like Russia's Putin and Venezuela's Chavez as they rose to authoritarian rule. In the hands of tyrants and demagogues, democracy and the rhetoric of patriotism or freedom are resignified to become political justification for imposing an authoritarian will which is against the best interests of the people.

We would be naïve thinking we dodged a bullet when Trump lost his reelection. True, Trump lost in 2020; but the loss failed to be satisfactory because a repudiation of four years of barefaced racism ("very fine people of both sides"), support for terrorist groups ("stand back and stand by"), promotion of sectarianism ("evil" and "crooked" Democratic lawmakers), sheer incompetency (almost 400,000 Covid deaths—over half preventable), pure stupidity ("disinfectant . . . knocks it out . . . is there a way we can do that . . . by injection"), and the weakening of the foundations of our democracy ("we're just not going to let [the vote certification] happen") did not occur. Four years of self-enrichment to the tune of $2.5 million of taxpayer money flowing to Mar-a-Lago and other businesses owned by Trump was not enough to repudiate the grifting of America.[11] Four years of lies and bullying failed to fulfill a hope that Trump would be totally and completely repudiated at the polls. As we know, a landslide election did not occur in 2020; instead, Trump came 21,461 votes from winning reelection.

During the presidential election coverage, shortly after Biden was declared the winner, CNN commentator Anthony Van Jones gave voice to the bittersweet victory. "There's the moral victory and there's the political victory, and they're not the same thing," he told his television audience. "I think for people who saw babies being snatched away from their mothers at the border, for people who are sending their kids into schools where the N-word is now being used against them, for people who have seen this wave of intolerance, they wanted a moral victory tonight. We wanted to see a repudiation of this direction for the country, and the fact that it's this close, it hurts. It just hurts."[12]

No longer being the Commander-in-Chief will not bring an end to the advances made among white supremacists during the four years of white rage. To make matters worse, white America is not even aware—and if aware uncaring—about the reestablishment of an apartheid society. Newly elected Joe Biden, after his return from his first European trip as president, boasted "America is back."[13] While reassuring to those less conservative Euroamericans who have experienced four years of trauma under Trump, for many relegated to the margins of whiteness, such proclamations are heard with a certain degree of angst. An America which is back—unchanged—is not good news for those who have been historically minoritized by such an America. There is no comfort in returning to the pre-Trump America. The greatest threat facing the United States is not a disruptive Russia, a competitive China, nor a rogue North Korea. But as Pogo once wisely stated: "We have seen the enemy and he is us." The most powerful and wealthiest empire ever known to humanity is being brought to its knees by a nationalist Eurochristianity, and the ignorance it fosters. Of course, this Eurochristianity, the spiritual justifier for the United States' perverted understanding of democracy, is not responsible for the original rise of Trump. He may have lost the 2020 presidential election, but his fervent supporters have only been energized by the rage of the loss of their political clout and an unfounded fear of those whom they have subjugated over the centuries gaining the political upper hand.

So, Trump leaving the White House is not the balm for what ails America. Failing to repudiate Trumpism means that the process of de-Trumpification cannot begin. And even if we try, it can never be repudiated until the white supremacist ideology that fostered it is recognized as evil and systematically purged from the dominant Eurochristian value system. Sadly, the failure to decisively repudiate Trumpism only emboldened those whom Trump calls patriots to embrace undemocratic strategies of overturning the will of the people, even if it means storming the Capitol and to hell with democratic principles. Despite legal attempts to overturn the will of the people, specifically the will of Black voters in Detroit, Atlanta, and Philadelphia, the Trump phenomenon came to an end on January 20, 2021. True, he remains influential in Republican politics; he may even run again in 2024. But regardless of any comebacks which may occur, Trump is not the cause of what ails the United States; he is but a symptom of white supremacy. Like the rest of us, he will one day breathe his last breath and become a dissertation topic for future academic projects focused on when the US empire began its steady decline, a cautionary tale about the fragility of democracy. The issue is not and never really was Trump. Thus, to solely focus on him ignores the unchallenged political and spiritual structures that can bring forth another future Trump-like rogue.

Let's be clear from the start of this book. Trump may very well be an irritating sore on the body politics of democracy, but he is not the cause of America's downward slide— even though he did accelerate the descent during his four years in office. A nation might reach imperial heights off the strength and sweat of an oppressed portion of its citizens, but such a model is unsustainable. If a house politically divided cannot stand, then a nation economically divided by those who are privileged and those who are relegated to fall short of their potential will also collapse. Like Jericho, such a nation is on the path toward implosion, as walls come crumbling down. The fault of Eurochristian nationalism does not solely lie with Trump nor Biden, Republicans nor Democrats. The white supremacist seeds of destruction have been sown into the very soil of our society ever since white feet touched Western Hemisphere lands, and its shoots continue to be nurtured and cared for to this day. Both Euroamerican liberals and conservatives are committed to the principles of apartheid. And while the former are adept at expressing white guilt and confessing a desire to do better, they, nevertheless, remain complicit with maintaining and sustaining this apartheid nation. True, conservatives are more odious as they cast themselves as the true victims of racism. And yes, liberals are less damning than conservatives, lacking solutions and the will to implement solutions even when they have the power to do so by capturing the presidency and both houses of Congress. In the final analysis, we are really left with a choice between bad and worse.

No doubt Trumpism continues to be based on heightened white anxiety and angst. Opportunity to explore possibilities for a more multicultural, justice-based social order has been lost. Diversity and a redistribution of power and wealth are defined as threats to Euroamericans rather than solutions in securing a more just and prosperous nation. The four years of collective PTSD caused by the Trump years have left many struggling with depression and desperation. Biden may very well be a reprieve from four years of madness; a moment to breathe before the rise of a Trump 2.0. The resilience of white supremacy is enough to make anyone hopeless. The future is indeed bleak.

Within the hopelessness of a Trumpian future, even if the person of Trump is absent from the equation, I write this manuscript. Those familiar with my work would recognize this book as the third of my *Badass* trilogy. The audience for the first book, *Burying White Privilege*, was Euroamericans. A clarion warning that Christianity was being strangled in the hands of Euroamericans, the book called for the death of their definition of Christianity, letting the dead bury the dead. An attempt was made to raise consciousness, an effort to hold Euroamericans responsible for their complicity with white supremacy, a complicity justified by their Eurochristian faith. The audience for the second book of this series, *Decolonizing Christianity*, was communities of color, an attempt to explore ways of decolonizing our minds. People of color contribute to their own oppression when they embrace Eurochristianity. Salvation can only be achieved when this Eurochristianity is rejected. This third and probably last book of the series which you hold in your hands attempts to play the prophet. With an eye on the past, it clearly sees we are heading toward the reemergence of a violent apartheid society. This book not only seeks to understand this phenomenon but engages in its resistance.

holy shit

2

The Reestablishment of an Apartheid America

Apartheid is the Afrikaans word for "apartness." When the National Party of South Africa gained political power in 1948, the white minority strengthened existing segregationist policies to intensify the plight of Blacks and Coloureds with harsher penalties and greater restrictions. With the election of Nelson Mandela in 1994, apartheid officially came to an end. Although the nomenclature "apartheid" is a modern term dating to the mid-twentieth century, the concept and strategy it signifies existed prior to the word. While the term "apartheid" has historically been linked to South Africa, it has provided a framework implemented by other minority populations whenever they grew fearful of a majority that might threaten or curtail the political power to which they have become accustomed. For example, America, since the first colonial settlers disembarked in Jamestown and Plymouth, designed a racial state based on "apartness."

As enslaved Blacks replaced white indentured servants, the racial and economic composition of the colonies changed. The original indentured servitude-based economy where poor whites worked for several years before being released from their vassalage transitioned to an enslaved Black-based economy. And even though Africans cost twice as much as an indentured servant, they were a better "investment" because they and their descendants perpetually remained property. During the first armed rebellion to take place in the colonies led by Nathaniel Bacon in 1676, indentured servants and the enslaved joined forces against the colonial white elites. Although the original intent of the uprising was fortifying the theft of indigenous land, with Bacon clamoring for the ruin and extirpation of Indians, it quickly morphed into securing the welfare of all classes living in the colony. The rebellion succeeded in chasing the colonial governor of Virginia, William Berkeley, out of Jamestown and burning the settlement to the ground.

By 1677 the rebellion was put down. Ruling white elites were concerned that poor whites and Blacks might again join forces against those economically exploiting them. A need developed to divide any commonalities between former poor white indentured servants and enslaved Blacks, an "apartness" if you will. A consequence of Bacon's Rebellion was the passage of laws that separated these natural allies by institutionalizing white supremacy. True, they may be oppressed indentured servants, but they were, after all, still white, and whiteness has its privileges. Such laws, a reaction to the fear of future alliances among poor whites and Blacks, protected privileged landholding elites from future threats to the social order they designed.

By 1680, three years after the end of the rebellion, the Virginia Assembly prohibited Africans and Indians from owning Christians (understood as white). Also, any non-Christians from Africa were to be enslaved for life. Eurochristians were granted permission to whip any enslaved or Black who dared confront a Christian. In 1682, conversion to Christianity would be insufficient for altering lifelong African servitude. The Virginia Slave Codes of 1705 further established white privilege and superiority. White indentured servants could no longer be whipped naked, only Blacks. They could also be dismembered if they were unruly. Blacks, even if they were free, were prohibited from owning guns. Whites could not be employed by Blacks who were free. All property (horses, cattle, and hogs) owned by those enslaved was confiscated and sold by the church with proceeds distributed among poor whites.[1] These segregationist policies, based on the construction of white supremacy to divide natural allies who shared economic oppression at the hands of an elite ruling class—who today we can call the "one percent"—has been an effective strategy throughout US history. However, today's possibility of a more racially just society threatens this social order. What is needed today is a new set of defenders of white supremacy to capture at least one of the two political parties if they hope to create a bulwark against the perceived threat of a post-racial America.

Political Party Realignments

The 1960s civil rights movement changed the political alliances of the two major parties. Until then, the Democrats were the party of slavery, the party of Jim and Jane Crow, the party of segregation. Republicans, the party of Lincoln, were seen as the party of emancipation, the party of Reconstruction. This explains why leaders for civil rights, like Frederick Douglass or Martin Luther King Jr., were Republicans—even though Republicans have had a history of selling out African Americans for political expedience. For example, Reconstruction came to a premature end because of a congressional bargain that ensured the Republican candidate, Rutherford Hayes, who lost the popular vote in 1876, would become president. In exchange, federal troops in South Carolina, Florida, and Louisiana were removed.

The current realignment occurred within the two political parties when the Southern Texan Democrat, Lyndon B. Johnson, signed the 1964 Civil Rights Act. According to legend, Johnson famously told an aide after the signing ceremony, "We have lost the South for a generation." His

Where is Reagan in this narrative?

apocryphal comments, if they were indeed made, fell short. Democrats lost the South for more than just one generation as segregationist Senators like Charles Pickering, Strom Thurmond, Thomas Wofford, Thad Cochran, Jesse Helms, and Trent Lott switched parties. This major realignment caused a shift in party alliances as African Americans became more loyal to the Democrats while white supremacist segregationists embraced Republicanism.

The 2016 presidential primaries were another watershed moment. We did not witness a political realignment like the one that occurred in the late 1960s; instead, a fracturing of the traditional Republican and Democratic Parties solidified. The Red America of Republicans and the Blue America of Democrats began to give way to a new political reality. At first it appeared as if the 2016 election would become a choice between representatives of the establishment, Jeb Bush for the conservative Reds and Hillary Clinton for the moderate Blues. While Reds and Blues approached government from different political worldviews, they would occasionally come together to negotiate in good faith for the betterment of America—that is, white America, of course. But since Newt Gingrich became the fiftieth Speaker of the House in 1995, an anti-bipartisanship was shepherded into the political arena as naked power became a means of retaining power. Take no prisoners became the mantra as "compromise" was seen as a dirty word. Bipartisanship gave way to government shut-

like? what? war? NAFTA? Big oil? Big pharma?

down in hard-knuckles politics, finding fruition in the gleeful denial of President Obama's Supreme Court nomination. And as the political climate changed, Blues like Obama and Biden pined for a bipartisanship of yesteryear.

Since the 1964 political realignment, the Blues were represented by figures like Lyndon B. Johnson, Jimmy Carter, the Clintons—Bill and Hillary—and Barack Obama. After the 2020 election, the Blues were led by Schumer in the Senate, Pelosi in the House, and Biden in the White House. They believe in a robust government charged with expanding opportunities to those shut out of the so-called American dream. Everyone deserves equal opportunities. Government, in their minds, exists to provide everyone with a fair shake. Health care is not an entitlement but a right. And for those who fall through the cracks, government has a responsibility to weave a safety net that can catch them. For them, affirmative action becomes one remedy for addressing historical racism. Although they may fundamentally believe in free markets, they believe retooling and reeducation are the means for how displacement caused by neoliberalism can be addressed. Because education and science are important, the coronavirus is dangerous, climate change is not a hoax, and the Covid vaccines work. Their vision of America is accomplished through laws such as the Build Back Better bill, which intended to redistribute the fruits of society concentrated in the hands of the few. Unfortunately, their cozy relationships with Wall Street hinders progress.

Urban, cosmopolitan, multicultural, and possessing advanced education, they believe in an America that is living into its mantra of "liberty and justice for all." They verbally reject prejudices while embracing the rhetoric of inclusion. However, for many who are supposedly represented by the Blues, especially people of color, the Democratic Party has fallen short. A feeling exists that while the rhetoric of inclusion might resonate, the Blue political class has not truly dealt with the liberal manifestation of racism that can be as insidious as the overt racism of the Reds. Despite any progressive legislation that might pass, people of color remain disillusioned because the political and business structures remain unjust and unfair as the tax burden lies heavily on the shoulders of the middle-class while the one percent can pay expensive CPAs to file returns that skirt their financial responsibility. Furthermore, the Blues have failed to truly grapple with the country's deindustrialization as global treaties continue to move high-paying jobs overseas. The service jobs that have replaced manufacturing jobs have led many—regardless of their higher education levels—to barely economically surviving. This has led many former union workers who were once loyal Democrats to switch to the Republican Party during the late 1970s. For many, the so-called American dream is relegated to mythology as the middle class continues to shrink.

The Reds became the primary voice of the Republican Party with the ushering in of the Reagan Revolution of the

1980s, solidified during the Bush dynasty. Political and religious conservatives, they believed in a muscular foreign
policy where America was called by God to be a shining
city upon a hill. White Protestants and Catholics flocked
to a worldview which distrusted government. This was not
a new phenomenon. Throughout American history, there
has always been a running anti-intellectual trend that distrusted government and education. Since America drank
from the New Deal fountain of social welfare and Keynesian
mixed-economy, Republicans perceived the nation to be in
decline. "Government," according to then-President Reagan,
"is not the solution to our problem, government is the problem."[2] He provided imaginary images of "strapping young
bucks" using food stamps to buy T-bone steaks and "welfare
queens" driving Cadillacs[3] to prove his point that government existed to help nonwhites. The education system,
since the elimination of prayer in school, was disastrous
as the nation increased its slide toward greater secularism.
Reds were fiercely anticommunist and held a strong aver-
sion to anything that smelled like socialism. Free-market
warriors in the vein of Milton Friedman, they advocated for
a limited government and cutting taxes. Deregulation and a
reverse form of Robin Hood created a cozy relationship with
corporate America.

Among the Reds' constituencies—those who are mainly
white with less formal education, mostly living in the rural

heartland far from the Blue coastal city dwellers—there was a sense that the America in which they grew up was being lost as their status—their power, privilege, and profit—was being threatened by those who since the foundation of the Republic resided on their margins. They felt left out from their rightful share of America, a birthright, as bank bailouts and corporate welfare contributed to a middle-class downward mobility. And yet, they were supposed to be what then-Vice Presidential nominee Sarah Palin would call the "real America."[4] While the political class among the Reds were reading intellectuals like William F. Buckley or George Will, the people were listening to ignoramuses like Bill O'Reilly and Tucker Carlson. Public intellectuals were replaced with injudicious opinion makers who based reality on supremacist illusions. Many of them began to find their voice during the rise of the late-2000 Tea Party Movement. The Republican Party thought they could ride the Tea Party tiger to political victories, only to find themselves being devoured by the very political allies they hoped to control.

The 2016 election was supposed to be an establishment coronation. In this traditional Red-Blue America, either Jeb or Hillary was destined to the throne. But unbeknownst to both sides of the same coin, America was undergoing a seismic political shift. Propelled by the 2008 Great Recession, unpayable student loans, and an inability to provide for oneself the bare basic necessaries of life (food, clothes, and

27

housing), both Blue and Red America began morphing as traditional Red-Blue rhetoric and orthodoxies failed them. One could argue that what developed was a postliberal and a postconservative worldview. The Blues started moving to what we can call a Liberative America while the Reds sought to reestablish an Apartheid America. Clinton came close to losing in the primaries to the representative of this emerging faction, Bernie Sanders. This Liberative America, often referred to as the progressive wing of the Democratic Party, is best illustrated by the House Squad,[5] which has yet to become a potent force. As of this writing, they find themselves in hand-to-hand combat with the Blues in creating a future America by means of the Build Back Better legislation.

Those aligned with bringing about a Liberative America are usually young millennials, who find themselves unable to match the financial security once enjoyed by their parents. While they may never have taken a critical race theory class, they nonetheless are familiar with the concepts of institutionalized racism, patriarchy, identity politics, and homophobia. They embraced #MeToo as a rebellion against both Red and Blue sexual predators and found the parade of police assassinations, which indicate Black lives fail to matter, as unacceptable. In response to these socio-political failings, they started moving toward a more collective, egalitarian response that challenged centuries of Eurocentric Enlightenment hyper-individualism. Many rejected the religion of their parents, repulsed by an apparent hypocrisy caused by the disconnect between the teaching of the church and the moral compass held by the younger generation. They tend, like the House Squad, to be women of color. Only time will tell if this vision of a Liberative America will capture the heart and soul of the Democratic Party, in the same way Apartheid America captured the Republican Party.

The shock of the 2016 election of Donald Trump was the rejection of the traditional Red America for an Apartheid America. He promised to make America great again by rejecting the Republican orthodoxy of Reds whom he dismissed with the pejorative term RINO (Republican In Name Only). This new political reality, however, is not necessarily new. What made America great in the past was that it was an apartheid nation since the late seventeenth century designed to benefit those who were considered white over and against all others. And while Trump ushered in this renewed reality, it has always been the predominate American modus operandi. Relegated to the fringes of the Reds, it has been centralized with a vengeance. After four years of Trump, Apartheid America hardened, vanquishing Reds who failed the "loyalty to Trump" litmus test. Xenophobia, sexism, and racism were no longer disqualifying positions for politicians, authoritarianism was no longer something to fear, vulgarity ceased being politically incorrect. We find ourselves in 2022 in an America where the Republican Party is a shadow of what they once were, taken over by those advocating an Apartheid America, while control for the Democratic Party rages between the Blues and those advocating for a Liberative America. Because those advocating for an Apartheid America captured the hearts and souls of one of the political parties, an expanding white supremacism is poised to become the driving force for the perceivable future.

Can't Be Racist—Voted for a Black Man

Notable Republicans, for some time, have denied the existence of racism in America. Former Vice-President Mike Pence during a 2021 speech hosted by New Hampshire Republicans described systemic racism as a "left-wing myth."[6] Senator Lindsey Graham (R-SC) proclaimed that same year on *Fox News Sunday* that "our systems are not racist. America's not a racist country."[7] Even Republican politicians of color have jumped on the bandwagon. Former ambassador to the United Nations Nikki Haley stated in 2020: "In much of the Democratic Party, it's now fashionable to say that America is racist. That is a lie. America is not a racist country."[8] Senator and race apologist Tim Scott (R-SC), during his response to President Biden's first address to the joint session of Congress, boldly proclaimed: "Hear me clearly, America is not a racist country."[9] And while Republicans are more vocal in their no-racism-exists assertion, Democrats have also expressed similar sentiments. President Joe Biden responding to Senator Scott agreed with him: "I don't think America is racist."[10] These white voices (even though some of the bodies from which they emanate contain high levels of melanin) perpetuate a lie, a lie safeguarded by legislation in some states prohibiting the critical teaching of American history. They insist any isolated horrors *some* people might have faced because of their skin pigmentation or ethnicity was not due to institutionalized oppression, nor due to structural racism, but instead due to individual biases and prejudices of a few bad apples. This is exactly the point made by Senator Graham when arguing America was not racist. He continued: "Within every society you have bad actors."[11]

Politicians peddle the myth of a racism-free nation because most Eurochristians believe people of color do not suffer more due to their race or ethnicity than white people. According to a 2020 study, 43 percent of Americans believe that the recent killing of Blacks by the police were isolated incidents rather than a systematic pattern. While 43 percent is a significantly high number, it gets worse when we consider that 79 percent of Republicans and most Eurochristians (70 percent evangelicals, 57 percent mainline Protestants, and 58 percent Catholics) agree with this assertion. And while most Americans (58 percent) might favor the goals of the Black Lives Matter movement, a minority of

Republicans (20 percent) do. When considering who faces greater discrimination, 71 percent of white evangelicals believe that discrimination against whites is as big a problem as the discrimination faced by people of color.[12]

If people of color do not face racism, then Euroamericans, by definition, cannot be racists. To vote for an unapologetic politician who spews racist comments does not, in their minds, indicate complicity with white supremacy. They can support a biased president by either (1) denying he really is racist; (2) apologizing, excusing, or explaining away his racism; (3) unashamedly applauding it; or (4) quietly supporting it. Support for Trump in 2016, in 2020, or today, regardless of the reasons given, is support of a person who said and did very racist things not just throughout his presidency, but throughout his life. Even if their support threatens democratic rule, support does not waver.

Support for openly racist political leaders, and commitment to a justice system undergirding white supremacy, transforms good churchgoing Eurochristians into barbarians. The history of white America has always been a history of savagery; a history of theft, of rape, and of decimation—all in the name of a white Christ. This is a genocidal history that spans from the 1637 Mystic massacre that resulted in the extermination of over four hundred Pequot men, women, and children; to the 1890 Wounded Knee massacre that resulted in the slaughter of over 150 Lakota men, women, and children; to Indian Schools where today we are unearthing the remains of children who died during a forced assimilation process of "kill the Indian and save the man."

This is a dehumanizing history that normalized that "peculiar institution," that kidnapped Africans to serve as chattel which could be economically exploited, maimed, raped, or killed; a "peculiar institution" whose power structures remained in place for a century after abolition through Jim and Jane Crow legislation. This included burning to the ground over twenty-five Black cities like Memphis (1866) and Tulsa (1921), or Philadelphia streets (1985), and a domesticating process where lynching, as a disciplinary technique geared to transform Blacks watching the punishment unfold into docile bodies, becomes a common occurrence. These subjugating techniques continue today through the rampant murder of African Americans by the police force because they have a broken taillight or have an air freshener hanging from the rearview mirror.

This is a blood-soaked history, from invading the countries of others through Manifest Destiny (Mexico and Puerto Rico) to steal their land; to invading the countries of others through Gunboat Diplomacy to steal their natural resources and cheap labor (the rest of Central America and the Caribbean basin); to Texas Rangers on horseback upon land which was previously Mexico, dragging the bodies of the original inhabitants behind them; to today tearing Brown children from their nursing mothers to be placed in cages and concentration camps on our southern borders, like the one in Tornillo, Texas. This is also an exclusionary history from the 1882 Chinese Exclusion Act that prohibited Asian immigration until 1943; to the 1885 Wyoming Chinese miners' massacre; to the establishment of Japanese internment camps during the Second World War as Japanese were fighting for America on the frontlines; to today's violence perpetuated and motivated by Trumpish proclamations of the "China virus."

The decimation of those who are defined as an affront to Eurochristianity, stereotyped as unrepenting beasts holding on to inferior cultures, continues to this day, but under more subtle methodologies where the violence ceases to be immediate and bloody but is instead drawn out and institutionalized. White supremacy ungirding the horrors implemented by humanity to secure a Eurochristian nation, even if today it does not necessarily result in the same bloodbaths of yesteryear, is nevertheless still responsible, in our present age, for putting people of color into early graves due to the wear and tear stress has upon their body. Even sympathetic liberal Euroamericans are complicit with white supremacy.

Can one blame people of color who refuse to trust Euroamericans, even when they are liberals? Refusing to reconcile with one's history, to even explore one's history in the classroom, maintains Euroamericans' complicity with white supremacy, less a matter of prejudices and more a consequence of ignorance. So, to answer Rodney King's question—No, we cannot all just get along. Why? Because the ultimate goal of white supremacy remains internally unchallenged, silencing all who fall short of whiteness by seeking the demise of their culture, to be replaced in some degree by assimilation. In short, to be a person of color living in the United States—then or now—is to live in fear, in danger, and under constant threat. No wonder whenever I find myself driving through a white neighborhood, I instinctively lock my car doors!

The Apartheid Gospel

Eurochristianity is utterly incongruent and incompatible with the teachings of Jesus Christ. When I argue that an inherent racism exists within Eurochristianity, it is easy to think of fringe groups who overtly tie white supremacy with the gospel message. Usually, we think of those on the extreme, like the Christian Identity movement that argued that only Germanic and Celtic people are God's chosen, the true descendants of Abraham, Isaac, and Jacob. Starting in the early 1970s, they facilitated the neo-Nazis in joining the Aryan Nation's compound near Hayden Lake in Idaho under the spiritual direction of Wesley and Lorraine Swift, who were eventually succeeded by Richard Girnt Butler of the Church of Jesus Christ-Christian. According to their teachings, the second coming of Christ would occur once the United States was restored as a white nation. Seldom is mainline Eurochristianity, which usually repudiates such extreme, ludicrous views, lumped with such explicit white supremacist groups. And yet, this book argues that all Eurocentric interpretations of Christianity are nevertheless detrimental, if not deadly, to communities of color regardless of how progressive or liberal Eurochristians might claim to be.

Eurochristianity—in both its conservative and liberal manifestations—has come to define self-interested subjective religious views as uncritical universal dogmas true for all humanity. Absent is any hermeneutical suspicion, skepticism of how the social location and context of Euroamericans contribute to the construction of faith and meaning. While expounding truth, consciously or not, Eurochristians reserve for themselves the divine right to define as moral whatever seems good in their own eyes, politically supporting whichever lie, theft, or death that advances their power, privilege, and profit. Political efficiency becomes the cornerstone of faith. Any harm that may befall the least of these is dismissed as collateral damage, a necessary evil in the quest for the common good—with "common" being a synonym for white. And yet, the gospel message core is a message of life. "I have come to give life and give life abundantly" (John 10:10).[13] Anything that brings death is, by definition, anti-gospel, contrary to the message and teachings of Jesus who insisted that every human, regardless of how lowly their earthly status might be, is created in the image of God and thus has dignity and the divine call to live a flourishing life.

If the gospel calls Christians to "life abundantly," then Eurochristian churches are not pro-life. No other people have been more committed to the instruments of death. Consider that the United States is the only nation in the world where the instruments of death—guns—outnumber civilians (120 for every 100 Americans)![14] US churches are silent about the major cause of death in this country (four gun-related deaths per 100,000 people), silent about self-inflicted harm (with only 4 percent of the global population, the United States accounts for 44 percent of worldwide suicides), and silent about mass shootings (half of industrialized countries reported at least one mass shooting between 1998 and 2019, with none reporting more than eight—in 2017 alone, the United States reported 561).[15] Christian politicians merged the symbols representing the birth of the Prince of Peace with the arsenal of Mars. Some, like Congresspersons Thomas Massie (R-KY) and Lauren Boebert (R-CO), posted photos of themselves and their children carrying semi-automatic weapons designed to kill multiple targets before their Christmas trees, days after a Michigan mass shooting. This bloodthirsty white Christ they insist is the reason for the season demonstrates an incongruency with any message that prioritizes "life, and life abundantly." Right to guns trumps right to life.

This Eurochristian culture of death goes beyond weapons of mass death. When churches advocate anti-vaxxer positions and encourage the nonuse of masks, they reveal themselves as apostles of death. When they remain silent in the face of death-dealing racism, ethnic discrimination, sexism, classism, and heterosexism—they foster a culture of death. Whenever they utter the name of Jesus, it becomes blasphemy rolling from their lips because of the disregard for life they harbor in their hearts. In their mouth, Jesus becomes an obscene word that disfigures the liberative teachings of the Gospels. If a tree is known by its fruit, then by their death-causing complicities, especially in relation to communities of color—historically and presently—they declare their allegiance to a non-prolife belief.

Eurochristianity provides their disciples spiritual justification to partake in savage inhumanity. This is a humanity lost by acting on the world stage in the name of a golden idol that wears the mask of a white, blue-eyed, blond Jesus. Followers of this false image will not discover their liberation or salvation while embracing Eurochristianity as truth. To bow one's knees to the God of whiteness and lead others to do likewise makes them—in the words of the apostle Paul: "false apostles, deceitful workers, masquerading as apostles of Christ. And no wonder, for Satan himself masquerades as an angel of light. It is not surprising, then, if his servants also masquerade as servants of righteousness. Their end will be what their actions deserve" (2 Cor. 11:13–15).

We are wrong to think Eurochristianity has anything to do with the message preached two thousand years ago by a colonized Brown rabbi on occupied land located at the margins of empire. Eurochristian nationalism is a political movement disguised in religious garb, a merger of death-inspired political and religious motifs. While it claims to worship the God of the Bible, it is not the God of the New Testament. It is also not the God that developed after the Babylonian captivity, nor the God before whom King David danced. Like humans, the biblical text has always revealed an evolving God. The God of Eurochristianity is like the tribal God of Exodus, Joshua, and Judges, the God of one people among the other Gods belonging to different tribes. One is commanded not to "worship any other Gods," but to be faithful to the God who led God's chosen into a Promised Land, a land already occupied by another people worshipping their own deities. Hence, because our God is more powerful than their God, the people are commanded to invade the land of others and kill everyone who draws breath (Josh. 6:17). The God who calls for genocide, who privileges God's chosen, has become the God of Eurochristianity.

In the hands of white settlers, such tribal Gods are dangerous. Passages calling for smashing the brains of the infants of one's enemy against rocks (Ps. 137:9) justifies the belief that the white God who led Europeans toward their own Promised Land calls for such violence against so-called devil-worshipping heathens and pagans. Like the chosen, the Godfearing men and woman of Jamestown and the Puritans of Plymouth had a moral obligation to exterminate everyone who drew breath and stood between them and the Promised Land, a land this Eurochristian God, through *his* ultimate love and mercy, provided for them.

To worship this tribal white God leads to feelings of exceptionalism, providing permission to break laws and participate in whatever act one defines as moral. Take Joshua Black, a Eurochristian from Alabama, arrested for his participation in the January 6th storming of the Capitol. When arrested, he told the FBI that "the Lord" wanted him to "plead the blood of Jesus" during the insurrection. Black claimed he was called by God to enter the Senate chamber and take up arms in the revolution, as needed.[16] In his mind, and those who are sympatico with his cause, believers are exempt from following the laws of the land because they are operating on God's orders—specifically the white nationalist tribal God who calls believers to subjugate the heathen liberals who surround them.

Who Is a Eurochristian?

Eurochristian is not an identity based on skin color nor faith tradition; it is an adherence to a worldview that privileges white supremacist ideology. This is a crucial point that if not understood early will make this book unintelligible. Although explained in my previous writings, this concept is so critical it requires reiteration. Ironically, advocates of white supremacy can be of any race or ethnicity. White skin pigmentation is not a prerequisite to be considered white. Because whiteness is a social construct and not a biological trait, proponents of racist policies are not solely those lacking melanin. In other words, what makes whiteness superior is not the biological but the social, a construct that assigns unearned power, privilege, and profit to those who possess white skin. Therefore, defenders of white supremacy can be Black, Latinx, Asian, or Indigenous. Think of Supreme Court Justice Clarence Thomas. True, such folk may not be considered white by the dominant culture. They would face, unless recognized, the same dangers others sharing their skin hue or ethnicity face. Still, they become in essence white, a useful tool in the advancement of white supremacy; their minds so colonized that they operate from and contribute to a worldview structure that privileges whiteness at the expense of Others who look like them.

A word of warning. Labels like oreo, coconut, banana, or apple are problematic when hurled at people of color who hold conservative political views. Communities of color are not monolithic; they hold diverse political positions. And while it is true that most people of color lean liberal, there are also those who vote Republican because they hold conservative religious views concerning hot-button issues like abortion, immigration, or neoliberal economic policies. It is one thing to have different perspectives on social issues, but it is an abomination to put on white face and say there is no racism in America so fellow conservatives can feel good about themselves. Worse is when people of color, either because of assimilation or a desire to belong, adopt and embrace white supremacy and its policies that remain death-dealing to those from their communities of origin.

As problematic as it is to legislatively deny the exploration of systemic racism in our education system, more damning is the total denial of racism. Of course, when white people deny the existence of racism, they are automatically looked upon with suspicion. What better way to polish the turd of racism than to have people of color doing the shining for them? What a gift to white Eurochristian nationalists to hear they are not racist from the mouths located on darker faces. The search is on to find a Black or Brown face who speaks with a white voice, easing any discomfort Euroamericans might experience due to their own unexamined complicity with racism. There were always those who acted against their own communities of origins. Let us not forget that there were Indians who served as scouts for the cavalry, leading them to decimate Indian villages. There were Blacks who tattled on those enslaved planning an escape from the plantation or a revolt. There were Jews who served in the Third Reich's military as soldiers and officers, some as field marshals and generals. Whether such persons are giving in to a survival instinct, self-hatred, submerged consciousness, pure opportunism, or any combination thereof, it is difficult to tell, making it too simplistic to provide an all-encompassing answer for their complicity. What leads and motivates them to betray their own people is complex and beyond the scope of this book to psychologically attempt to determine. Enough for now to recognize there are people of color who are committed to Eurochristianity.

And just as Eurochristianity is not exclusively comprised of whites, it is also not exclusively comprised of Christians. Disciples of Eurochristianity are not just multiracial and multiethnic, they also hail from different faith traditions, or no faith tradition at all. Those benefitting from whiteness need not be Christian, for they can still be privileged because of the dominant Eurochristian worldview. They may be atheists, Jews, humanists, Muslims, or agnostics. Regardless of their faith tradition, or lack thereof, the overall dominant white supremacy that creates a neat dichotomy between white and Black makes those who can pass as white into honorary Eurochristian atheists, Eurochristian Jews, Eurochristian humanists, Eurochristian Muslims, or Eurochristian agnostics. Remember, Eurochristian has nothing to do with a set of beliefs or dogmas; it has to do with spiritually justifying white supremacy's colonizing tendencies.

Can Euroamericans Be Saved?

In my previous writings I asked the reader to imagine the absurdity of approaching a domestically abused spouse to hold them accountable for failing to gently approach their abuser with solutions to prevent future beatings. The abused is prohibited to speak through tears or in anger, for such passionate responses are quickly dismissed as being "too emotional." We expect the one with blackened eye and the split lip to provide a rational resolution to their predicament, a way forward that does not make the abuser feel bad about themselves. The responsibility falls upon the persecuted to craft a response to their suffering in loving-kindness lest the tormentor feel threatened, guilty, or uncomfortable. Those privileged by the abusiveness of white supremacy expect those who for centuries have been slapped around to provide the solution for disenfranchisement and the balm that soothes the batterer's troubled soul. Do you see how absurd it is to expect the violated partner in the relationship to fix the relationship?

Because this abusive relationship is so entrenched, we must ask if it is beyond reformation. Can Eurochristianity be saved? Has its complicity with white supremacy, patriarchy, and colonialism made it totally irreconcilable with any gospel message of liberation? This book—and the two others that preceded this one—argues that the Christianity that developed within the United States is beyond redemption. The faith of Euroamericans that has justified centuries of bloodshed and oppression can never be atoned for until every tear wept by an undocumented child encaged in a border concentration camp is accounted for, until every person murdered by the police for driving while not white is expiated, until every piece of stolen land is returned. Who can offer forgiveness for centuries of blood drawn by the whip, the noose, the bullet? Certainly not the descendants of those massacred in the past. How presumptuous to imagine today's marginalized communities can speak for their ancestors, that they are empowered to offer redemption in their names. Those who have been slaughtered are the ones who must rise from the dead and offer forgiveness. Until then—there exists no mechanism by which forgiveness can be offered.

Eurochristianity is beyond salvation. Even Euroamericans realize the inability of Eurochristianity to save as a majority leave the church. For the first time in US history, more adults do not attend or belong to a house of worship than those who do. According to yearly Gallup poll surveys, religious affiliation since 1939 never dipped below 68 percent throughout the twentieth century. With the start of the new millennium, religious membership has been steadily dropping, reaching 47 percent by 2020.[17] Religion in general, Eurochristianity particularly, is dying, becoming irrelevant. While many reasons might exist for this agnostic drift toward secularism—pedophilic priests, homophobic stances, misogynist views—no doubt a major contributor, according to a ten-year in-depth study conducted from 2000 to 2010, is the political actions and attitudes of religious people. A backlash against the Religious Right has resulted in an exodus, contributing to the steady demise of Eurochristianity. Fascinating to note that the study discovered that higher rates of the religiously unaffiliated were more common in Republican-controlled states. Whenever the Christian Right was more active and publicly vocal concerning hot-button political issues, more people self-identified as having no religious affiliation.[18]

To be a Eurochristian has come to mean loyalty to 45. The greatest indicator that an individual will cast their vote for a Trumpish political agenda is their whiteness and having a religious affiliation, especially if they claim to be evangelicals.'The hope for a more just America, one that truly moves away from its racist, sexist, and homophobic past, is the growth of the religiously unaffiliated. Can you appreciate the irony of what I just wrote? I, a person who has dedicated his adult life to the good news of the gospel, an ordained minister, am calling for the demise of a manifestation of Christianity for the sake of justice, for the sake of liberation, for the sake of humanity. Calling for the death of Eurochristianity does not mean a call for an end to spirituality. In fact, I choose to continue the embracement of mystery, the embracement of the unknown, the embracement of divinity—an embrace that can never occur if society insists on bowing their knees to the golden idols of Eurochristianity. These idols and their religious and political enablers require complete and total rejection. Eurochristian nationalism must be discredited and discarded if there is to be any hope for liberation and salvation.

How then can Euroamericans who follow what James Cone has called a satanic Christianity ever find their salvation in a religious tradition that has planted the seeds of its own destruction? What hope is there for those who continue today to benefit because of the Eurochristian race-based actions taken by supremacist ancestors? Obviously, they are not guilty for what their ancestors did. They are not guilty if their ancestors were Indian killers, masters of the enslaved, invaders, and colonizers. They are guilty of continuing to benefit from the unearned power, privilege, and profit gained due to the social structures their forebears established. They are guilty of maintaining and sustaining white supremacy. They are guilty of thanking God for their blessings when those so-called blessings have been obtained because of the extracted sweat, blood, and tears of those relegated to the underside of whiteness. They are guilty of continuing to worship this white God who offers amnesia for the conquest, invasion, and colonialism that was called for in *his* name.

As argued in the two earlier books of this series, killing this white God, renouncing this Eurochristianity, and learning to bow one's needs to the God of the oppressed is the only hope for Euroamericans' salvation. There are no white supremacists in Heaven. Period. Salvation comes with the crucifixion of whiteness on the crosses of patriarchy, racism, ethnic discrimination, homophobia, classism, colonialism, and heterosexism. Eurochristianity must die so that in its place a new creature can be born again. Unfortunately, most have yet to realize this truth. So I'll say it again—let the dead bury the dead!

3

An Apartheid Eurochristian Genealogy

How does the original gospel message of love get perverted to become a justification for the barbarism inflicted in Christ's name during the quest for white supremacy? How do those hailing from Europe replace Jews to become the new Israel, the new chosen people? More important than abstract arguments for the existence of God is the character of this God who we claim exists. But what if this God who we insist exists happens to be white? Specifically, a white male. If power creates faith, dogma, and religion, then faith, dogma, and religion justify power. The creation of God in the image of male whiteness embraces a deity designed to protect and preserve the unearned privilege, power, and profit designated for those who possess—like their God—white penises. This is the real problem of Eurochristianity, God's white penis, under whose shadow humanity has been oppressed. A white male God exists to serve, protect, and bless all who share similar endowments. Prayers are lifted by these God creators to the heavens; prayers to have more, transforming their deity to an Amazon distribution center geared to filling orders. Belief in this white male God, acceptance of the white Jesus as a personal Lord and Savior, and faithfulness to white theology creates the greatest threat facing Christianity while simultaneously being life-denying to communities of color.

Sadly, many who hail from the global South have been forced to live under the worse form of tyranny, the oppressiveness of their colonialized minds, conditioned to seek their liberation through the Eurocentric theologies and philosophies responsible for their oppression. To bow one's knees to this white male God and the Eurochristianity *he* represents is to become complicit with a political ideology designed—since its foundation—to carry out the decimation of all who fall short of male whiteness. Embracing Eurochristianity, especially by those this spirituality is designed to colonize, legitimizes white supremacy in the minds of the colonized while normalizing complicity with the Eurocentric violence and terror historically unleashed upon the global South and their migrating descendants.

If you are an African American Christian, you can thank slavery. If you are a Native American Christian, you can thank the settlement of your lands by Europeans. If you are an Asian Christian, you can thank Pacific colonialism. The Christianity practiced by so many US communities of color is a consequence of Europeans decimating their ancestors. Those victimized due to the imposition of Eurochristianity have lived for centuries under the mercy of those who have historically proven to lack mercy. Every descendant of a people once defined as subhuman by Europeans owes it to their forebears to ask why they are Christians. Are they betraying their progenitors by bowing their knees to the religion responsible for so much suffering and misery faced by their predecessors?

Over the centuries, Eurochristianity has fostered a culture of cruelty, a culture of death that bows its knees before the cult of violence. In the name of their white Christ, Cristobal Colón ordered the noses of the Taíno people to be cut off for refusing to submit to colonial authority. His *conquistadores* would place bets on their ability to slice off a limb or a head with simply one blow of their sword; or they just threw *indios* to their dogs to be torn apart. In the name of their white Christ, the US cavalry attacked peaceful Cheyenne and Arapahoe following US instructions by settling in an area called Sand Creek. They were mainly women, children, and the elderly. After the unprovoked massacre, they were scalped to obtain souvenirs to be shown off at the Denver saloons. Soldiers cut off White Antelope's ears and nose as trophies. One of the soldiers who was present wrote about the tobacco pouch made of pieces of skin cut from the genitalia of the dead. In the name of their white Christ, and under the personal rule of King Leopold II of Belgium, the Congolese were forced to collect natural rubber. If they failed to meet their quota, they were shot. But to account for each bullet spent, soldiers had to provide proof by producing the severed hand of the victim. Many, in an attempt to stockpile expensive bullets, indiscriminately cut off hands of the living. In the name of their white Christ, African Americans were consistently lynched and mutilated during church picnics. At the last moments of life, good churchgoing Christians would descend upon the body to cut off pieces to keep as souvenirs. Photos were taken to mark the festive occasion. The message of love preached by Jesus and the savage and sadistic practices of Eurochristianity are irreconcilable.

What is the point of faith in the absence of love and justice? How can those who suffered vicious and malicious horrors at the hands of Eurochristians become its disciples? To put on white face by learning white theology, practicing white ethics, worshipping to white liturgy, and interpreting the Bible through white hermeneutics ignores the cry of ancestors and makes us complicit with the social and political structures responsible for our own oppression. Every Latin American child thrown into a cage, every Black life that did not matter that meets its end during a minor traffic violation, every Asian beaten up for supposedly carrying the coronavirus, and every Indian living in Third World conditions on their own land is perpetrated by those who worship this white Jesus and follow this Eurochristian nationalism.

A problem exists with the Jesus that developed within Eurocentric culture that understands itself as God's chosen with the privilege of gazing upon all who fall short of the glory of whiteness, defining them as less-than. Decolonizing Christianity requires forsaking, rejecting, and repudiating whiteness and the Eurochristian religion that has for centuries spiritualized white supremacy. We are left wondering if there is something unchristian about Christianity. From its beginnings, Eurochristianity seamlessly evolved into an ideology at odds with the original message of Jesus Christ. Communities forced to exist on the underside of Christianity, due to centuries of oppression, may have rejected the message and teachings of Jesus because of how Eurochristians misinterpreted and misused the Gospels. And so be it—they are not to blame. Saying no to Jesus may be the only path to healing and should be encouraged. Others—like myself—may be attracted to the message of liberation found in Jesus's teachings while rejecting what Christianity has become. But if those of us on the margins of whiteness truly desire to become followers of this gospel message, regardless of all the harm, all the theft, all the death imposed by Eurochristianity, then we must reject the latter before we can ever embrace the former. To be a follower of Jesus's message is to become an enemy of Eurochristianity and participate in its destruction.

But can those whose ancestors suffered at the hands of Euro-christian nationalism ever claim the teachings of Jesus without betraying their forebears? For some, the scars are too deep, and the wounds have festered for too long so that it becomes impossible. For others who find themselves situated in the in-between space, residing in the contradiction of competing cultures, embracing Jesus's teachings while rejecting Eurochristianity may be possible, even healing. Latinx thinkers—specifically Chicanos—have referred to this "in-between" space by employing the Aztec term *nepantla*. Jorge Klor de Alva has understood *nepantla* to mean "that situation in which a person remains suspended in the middle between a lost or disfigured past and a present that has not been assimilated or understood."[1] For many, *nepantla* focuses on that in-between space where Latinxs, specifically those with First Nation roots, deny neither their indigenous customs and traditions nor the spiritual manifestations created and caused by the violent vicissitudes of conflicting cultures; where consequently, the blood of the conquered and the conquerors flows through their veins.

For many of us, we belong to multiple cultures—none of them fully accepting us. We are too American to ever fit in our cultures of origin, a truth reinforced whenever we visit the lands of our origins. And of course, we are too ethnic and/or our skin pigmentation is too dark to ever belong in Euroamerica. Residing in the betweenness of *nepantla* forces us to recreate our own culture from elements of the societies that find agreement in defining us as their bastards. In this in-between space, for some of us (obviously not all—nor should it be all) we find the teachings of another colonized person—Jesus—instructive. He had to survive under Rome as we who currently exist under the American Rome. But before we choose to follow the message and teachings of this colonized man called Jesus, we first really need to know what we are rejecting; if not, then all rebuffing is reduced to rhetoric. This chapter will explore the philosophical development of Eurochristianity, a Christianity that made a preferential option for whiteness and in the process fostered a culture of cruelty.

No doubt some, especially defenders of Eurochristianity, will bristle at the brevity concerning the major intellectual contributors listed below. They would be correct in noting that the summaries are too concise, too elementary, focus too narrowly on just one aspect of their prolific writings. Obviously, the works of these thinkers are much broader. Entire books can be written—and they have—on their entire oeuvre. But that is not the purpose of this brief literary review. The focus is not even on what they *actually wrote*. More important, for our purposes, is how the Christianity they helped shape has been interpreted and/or misinterpreted by Eurochristians to fortify white supremacy.

The Problem with Paul

Paul (4?–62/67? CE), like all humans, was a product of his culture and time whose worldview, like ours, was affected and impacted by the philosophical conversations occurring during his lifetime. We know Paul, the Roman citizen, was a colonized man who was also known as Saul, the Jewish Pharisee. What we can deduce about this historical man is that he too existed in *nepantla*—if such a term would have existed during his time. How he came to understand the gospel message of Jesus was strongly influenced by his Jewishness, interpreted through the lens of Greek and Roman thought. As he preached his understanding of Jesus's message based on his social location, others, with similar backgrounds, came to embrace the Christianity that he was evangelizing. So much so that his interpretation of Jesus's message has become vital, as future generations of scholars and believers quoted and misquoted his writings.

In the "what if" of history, we can only imagine how the gospel message would have been different if Paul had made a right turn at Macedonia, as he originally intended, rather than a left due to his vision (Acts 16:6–10). Maybe Christianity would have come to be understood through Hindu and Buddhist concepts rather than Greco-Roman thought. But a left turn he made, and because of his own intellectual formation and the locale from where he preached, the Semitic worldview that birthed Christianity was transformed by a Greco-Roman perspective. For example, early Christian writers like Paul were highly influenced by the platonic concept of the body/soul duality—specifically the preexistence and immortality of the soul. Unlike Judaism that preached the oneness of human nature and thus bodily resurrection (Dan. 12:2), Paul advocates for the split between the mortal body and the immortal soul.

Also, more aligned with Stoicism than Jesus, Paul devalues the body, arguing flesh was conceived as being corruptible, while only the spirit can grasp the eternal. "Flesh and blood are unable to inherit God's kingdom," he writes, "nor does corruption inherit incorruption" (1 Cor. 15:50). Stoic emphasis on seeking inner peace through the human will's ability to control passions contributed to a negative view of the body, specifically sexual desire. For stoics an indifference exists toward sex. Marriage required self-control as the purpose for sex became procreation.

As other scholars have noted, Paul's admonition concerning sexual "misconduct" in the first chapter of Romans parallels *Epistle 95*, the missive of the most celebrated Stoic thinker of his time, Seneca, a mentor and advisor to Emperor Nero. For Seneca, divine reason was the only hope to transform Rome, which had descended into moral debauchery, specifically sexual misconduct. Romans 11:18–32 specifically is replete with resonances of Seneca's moral philosophy, a possible attempt by Paul to broaden the appeal of the gospel.[2] Because the flesh was inherently sinful, believers became alienated from their bodies. Redemption is found when the sinner flees the sinful influences of their body by forsaking

Explain

earthly pleasures. Paul reminds us: "The fact is that I know that in me, that which is in my flesh, dwells nothing good, for while the desire to do good is present, in practice I cannot find the good. . . . What a wretched man I am! Who will deliver me from this body of death? . . . So then I with my mind truly serve God's law, and with the flesh the law of sin" (Rom. 7:18, 24, 26). Holiness was achieved through self-denial, where the believer concentrated on things of the spirit rather than of the flesh, a theme that has plagued Christianity in general, Eurochristianity specifically.

Punishing the body glorifies the spirit. And what better way to cast out the corruption of bodies than pain—think of self-flagellation as a spiritual disciplinary form of devotion geared to mortify the flesh. Consider St. Benedict (480–543 CE), founder and abbot of the Citadel of Camoania monastery, who was gripped with sexual desire, lusting for a woman he once gazed upon. Fearful he would abandon his hermit calling, he

> noticed a thick patch of nettles and briers next to him. Throwing his garment aside he flung himself into the sharp thorns and stinging nettles. There he rolled and tossed until his whole body was in pain and covered with blood. Yet, once he had conquered pleasure through suffering, his torn and bleeding skin served to drain the poison of temptation from his body. Before long, the pain that was burning his whole body had put

out the fires of evil in his heart. It was by exchanging
these two fires that he gained the victory over sin. So
complete was his triumph that from then on, as he later
told his disciples, he never experienced another temp-
tation of this kind.[3]

If self-imposed physical punishment leads one closer to
God, would it not then be an act of love and mercy to impose physical punishment on other sinners? Does meting
out inquisitional type torture provide spiritual liberation for
the sinner or unbeliever? If so, then Paul, while not calling
for the infliction of pain on others, nonetheless laid the Eurochristian groundwork of exacting pain, institutionalizing
violence as a Christian discipline, if not virtue.

The problem with Paul is not how his social location
changed the gospel message of Jesus. After all, when a religion enters a new culture, both the culture and the religion
are bound to change, neither ever staying the same. The
problem with Paul is that his culturally inspired understanding of the gospel message, specifically his foundational
Greco-Roman philosophical thought that would eventually
give rise to Eurocentrism, came to be equated with the Logos,
the Word of God. To read Paul is not to read the specific interpretations of a historical man situated in the very early stages
of what would become Eurocentrism. To read Paul is supposedly to read the mind of God. This becomes highly dangerous

because the Eurocentrism that is built on the Greco-Roman philosophical foundation justifying inflicting pain is perceived as having divine origins. We are no longer wrestling with some culture's worldview, we are wrestling with God, and as such, to reject this developing Christianity is to become an enemy of God, licensing the faithful to eliminate, if necessary through the implementation of pain, those who dare stand against God. The problem with Paul is that future Eurochristians accepted a corrupt flesh, a despised body.

The Problem with Justin Martyr

To oppose God's anointed is to be demonic, to be in league with the forces of evil. Following in Paul's footsteps, among the earliest *correlationists* seeking to reconcile the gospel message of Jesus with Greco-Roman thought was the second-century Greek apologist Justin Martyr (100-165 CE). Among the first Christian philosophers, he was well-versed in Platonic and Stoic thought, beginning the first Christian school in Rome where he offered a defense before the empire for the Christian faith he was shaping. Influenced by Philo of Alexandria (25? BCE-50 CE), Justin argued that the moral truths discovered in Platonism and Stoicism found their most complete expression in the teachings of Jesus because they were attuned to the wisdom of the Logos—meaning both word and reason—even though these Greco-Roman thinkers were not familiar with the teachings of

Jesus. Any truth dimly known by Plato and others was due, even before the incarnation, to the revelation of the Logos, making Plato and other pagans anonymous Christians, a là Karl Rahner (to use a more modern term).

By connecting God's incarnation in Christ—literally the Word (reason) becoming flesh (John 1:14)—with the Stoic concept of the divine Logos found in the hearts of all humans, Justin concluded Christianity was the only true religion whose moral doctrines were exclusively valid since the foundation of human existence. What was partially known by former philosophers is now fully known by Christians. If Christianity is the only true religion, then ipso facto, all other religions must be false; but not just false, satanic. He writes, "wicked devils perpetrated these [other religions]. And we are taught that only those are deified who have lived near to God in holiness and virtue; and we believe that those who live unjustly and do not change their ways are punished in eternal fire."[4] The father of lies, Satan, is responsible for leading humanity away from the truth of the Logos by way of false religions that deny the universality of Jesus's incarnation. Any wisdom learned after the incarnation that was outside Christianity, discovered among nonbelievers, was dismissed as a perverted fragment of the Truth (with a capital "T"), a perversion that occurred due to Satan and his demons.

With time, missionary conquerors would encounter the faith traditions of people in Asia, Africa, and the Americas. The religions, worldviews, and/or philosophies of those who would become the colonized were, by definition—thanks to Justin Martyr—satanic. Once a way of life is demarcated as the product of evil, Eurochristianity believed it had a moral obligation, a literal calling from God, to eradicate falsehood and if need be, those who refuse to renounce their so-called evil practices. Justin Martyr's writings not only provided the religious justification for imperial conquest, but by designating the faith of others as demonic, he provided moral justification to eradicate all those who refused to bow their knees to Jesus and, by extension, those claiming to be his disciples. Even today one hears the echoes of Justin Martyr in the pronouncements of Euroamerican Christians.

When a radio host asked evangelical leader Franklin Graham why he thought people were trying to undermine then-President Trump, Graham replied: "Well, I believe it's almost a demonic power that is trying."[5] Paula White, Trump's spiritual advisor credited with leading Trump to Christ, kicked off his reelection campaign with prayer: "Right now, let every demonic network who has aligned itself against the purpose, against the calling of President Trump, let it be broken, let it be torn down in the name of Jesus!" She added: "I declare that President Trump will overcome every strategy from hell and every strategy from the enemy—every strategy—and he will fulfill his calling and his destiny."[6]

One is not simply politically wrong for disagreeing with Eurochristian nationalism; one is evil, possessed by the devil. When we consider the majority of those who opposed Trump were from communities of color, then it must be concluded they are satanic, enemies of God's truth manifested as white religion and philosophy. Justin Martyr is updated as Eurochristians following God's will seek to dismiss, disenfranchise, and demonize those who oppose their white supremacist political views. Dismissing the Others as infernal has historically provided license to physically wipe out such evil from their midst. And here is the dilemma for those defined as evil—can they ever truly reconcile with those bent on eradicating them? The problem with Justin Martyr is that his writings justified future Eurochristians to define those who were not Christians as demon worshippers.

The Problem with Augustine of Hippo

The nascent church looked to the heavens for their King. Proclaiming that the emperor was not the ultimate authority was a threat to his rule. Religion that places God over the state must either be eradicated or domesticated. At first, the state participated in multiple persecutions of Christians, from being thrown to wild beasts in the Roman arenas to serving as human torches in the gardens of Nero. But with time, the faith was captured by the State in a marriage of convenience. For a divided empire, an official religion created unity and justification. God brought forth the empire for *his* glory and purpose. For the faith, protection was offered from interpretations perceived as wrong as a powerful political structure existed to crush religious opposition. Unfortunately, Christianity ceased being an article of faith when it became the ideology that justified the empire—as it did in 313 CE.

Constantine (274–337 CE), one of the four emperors of a divided domain, began a military campaign to make Rome great again through unification. The night before the Battle of the Milvian Bridge in 312 CE, Constantine dreamt Christ was instructing him to place a Christian sign (a monogram combining the first Greek letters, X and P, of Christ's name) on the shield of his soldiers, although the historian Eusebius claims he saw a vision in the sky with the words "In this conquer." Regardless as to how the revelation occurred, the result was the same. What was originally the signifier for the Prince of Peace (☧) became, for the first time, a symbol for war, death, and conquest. Constantine attributed his victory to the God of the Christians, superficially converting to the faith. And while he proclaimed himself "bishop of bishops," he continued to serve as a high priest to other Gods, even having the Senate, upon his death, declare him a God. Christianity was not so much a matter of fervent belief, but imperial opportunity.

By 313 CE, with the signing of the Edict of Milan, Constantine legislated the tolerance of Christianity, a relief after decades of persecution by Roman authorities. Soon, the church became an imperial tool to advance political policies. Imperial ideologies were imposed upon the church's theology, softening the radical biblical pronouncements against worldly powers and principalities. With time, Christianity became dependent on political powers and in return became its apologist. By the time of Augustine of Hippo (354–430 CE), the once mighty Rome was in decline. As a young man he was familiar with the infamous Battle of Adrianople in August 378 CE when Rome lost to the Goths. Later in life, in August of 410 CE, he experienced the consequences of the sacking of Rome by the Visigoths over a three-day period.

Many saw the pillaging of Rome as punishment by the traditional Roman Gods because the civil authorities abandoned them and instead embraced Christianity. Augustine responded by writing *The City of God* (426 CE). Christianity was not why Rome was plundered; quite the contrary, it was responsible for its success.[7] Although the empire once was an instrument of Christian persecution, Augustine believed it now existed to spread, secure, and protect Christianity. He concluded God allowed the mighty Roman Empire to exist to accomplish God's will of using its roads and civic organizations to spread Christianity throughout the world.[8] And even if Rome—the earthly city—was to one day fall (as it eventually did in 476 CE, some forty-six years after Augustine's death), what was more important was the ultimate triumph of the City of God.

CHAPTER 3

For Augustine, there exist two distinct cities—the City of God formed by the love of God and the City of Humans formed by the sinful nature of human self-love. The former represents the heavenly abode where saints live in perfect and eternal harmony with the divine while the latter is the abode where wickedness rules according to the standards of the flesh.[9] But how do those wishing to govern according to God's principles rule in the reality of a sinful city, especially when they are charged to maintain civil order, a civil order that at times requires the threat, fear, and implementation of punishment? Yes, it would be great to live in accordance with the principle of love that rules the City of God, but in the City of Humans, correction by fear is more effective. Rulers of empires are not called to lead souls to act according to the principles of the City of God (that is the role of the church), but to constrain wickedness.[10] Providing an argument for the need of and importance of the City of Humans, the original pacifist gospel message moved further from the call to love and seek peace, even to the point of creating a just war theory. The Constantination of Christianity was made possible when Christian "fathers" of the faith like Augustine looked to the empire to serve as the supporter and defender of the faith, and in return, the faith became the justifier of the empire— during the time of Augustine and during our own time.

What Augustine proposed would have dire consequences for Christianity as the Pope, with armies of his own, became

Augustine to Hitler?

a political figure crowning kings during the Middle Ages, rather than a moral authority. When the political fortunes of the church turned, as they did in 1309 when the French king moved the papacy to Avignon located in France, the church became an imperial tool to enrich secular rulers. When the church becomes a political player, it bends to the will of the state to secure whatever power the state carves out for it. Take the recent examples during the Second World War when the church, rather than being a witness against the human rights violations (especially the genocidal policies aimed at the Jews) being experienced at the hands of fascists, instead signed the 1929 Lateran Treaty that recognized the dictatorship of Mussolini in exchange for papal sovereignty over Vatican City. Or the *Reichskonkordat*, which guaranteed the right of the church to operate in Germany if bishops, upon taking office, took an oath of loyalty to the Nazi regime. The problem with Augustine is that he developed a theological justification that facilitated Eurochristian rulers using the church to advance their secular political goals.

The Problem with Origen, Anselm, and Abelard

Christianity is a bloody faith. The emphasis is on shedding blood, specifically the blood of the innocent. Jesus's bloody crucifixion is seen as the act by which salvation is achieved. This idea of being saved by the blood of the lamb developed over centuries. Origen (184?–254?) was among the first to wrestle with the meaning of the crucifixion, developing a theory of the atonement. For him, Jesus fooled Satan by appearing weak during his crucifixion and getting access to the Devil's domain, only to defeat Satan when he gave him (per Matthew 20:28) "his own soul as a *ransom* on behalf of many," returning victorious from the dead.[11] This ransom is paid for all who have and will die, creating the way to follow Jesus from death to life. It was Anselm of Canterbury (1033?–1109) who first developed the theology of satisfaction. Jesus's death was not to pay a ransom to the Devil as per Origen, but to satisfy the loss of God's honor. Humans' sinfulness required punishment. Unable to procure a proper atonement, God initiates the process by which humans can find salvation through an ultimate sacrifice. Finite beings cannot offer satisfaction to an infinite being. Only the self-sacrifice of a sinless God-as-human can make restitution and restore God's honor.[12] According to Abelard (1079–1142), a younger contemporary of Anselm, Jesus neither paid a debt to the Devil nor to God. Instead Abelard insisted God demonstrated through the sacrificial offering of *his* only begotten child, *his* exemplary love that serves as the basis for atonement and reconciliation, providing humanity with the opportunity to respond to God's mercy. Such love moves humans to respond likewise, moving God to forgive.[13]

Jesus's crucifixion as a ransom either to God or the Devil, or as a demonstration of God's love, is achieved by the tortuous, gory, and bloody death of Jesus, a cosmic form of child abuse. Humans can avoid what they deserve, the righteous wrath of God as per Origen and Anselm, by obtaining salvation through the sacrificial and substitutional blood that cleanses, or experience the depth of God's love through the blood that cleanses. This is a gift, an unearned gift freely given on the cross to satisfy God. But if true, then death and suffering become salvific, the way one reaches God. The problem with such a theology as developed in Eurocentric thought is that those wishing to imitate Jesus are taught that pain, humiliation, and abuse are salvific, the price of discipleship, which entails picking up one's cross and following. The poor of the world, those abused by the structures that privilege the dominant culture, are taught that their reward is in the hereafter, not the here-and-now. What they suffer now will be offset by what awaits them after death. Suffering for Jesus—and for the disenfranchised—becomes redemptive. But as many womanist scholars have reminded us, there is nothing salvific about suffering. Any doctrine that honors and glorifies suffering encourages a type of quietism where pain is stoically borne. Instead of seeking to change the oppressive status quo, acceptance of oppression becomes God's will, the means of obtaining grace, and more importantly to crucifiers, maintaining the social structures that fortify the dominant culture.

Besides domesticating individuals on the margins, substitution theology (I should have been crucified, but instead Jesus took my place) reinforces global Eurocentric supremacy. The Euroamerican elites, with a globally expanding neoliberalism, demand sacrificial lambs to be led to the economic slaughterhouse. Unfortunately, these lambs mostly hail from the global South and communities of color within the empire. To satisfy this white God, instigators of free markets offer up bodies from the economic periphery as living sacrifices, producing riches so Euroamericans can have life, and life abundantly. For whites to be blessed by the white God, those on their margins must be relegated to suffering and death, a ransom paid so the elect can enjoy their economic salvation. The Eurochristian doctrine of substitution condemns those on the underside of history. If their God-given status is threatened by concepts like democracy or equality, then such concepts are violently fought against as being demonic manifestations of the opposite of God's will—socialism.

But what if crucifixion is not salvific? What if crucifixion is understood as Jesus's radical solidarity with the countless multitudes of history who continue to be lynched on the crosses of hatred, the crosses of racism, the crosses of sexism, the crosses of ethnic discrimination, the crosses of heterosexism, and the crosses of classism? The idea of pacifying a God offended by human sin makes God a snowflake. The importance of the cross for those marginalized by white supremacy is that a God exists who fully understands the trials and tribulations the world's wretched face because Jesus, God-in-the-flesh, also suffered trials and tribulations. The world's disenfranchised have a Jesus who understands their sufferings.

The Problem with the Sacredness of Blood

Because Christianity is a bloody faith, Eurochristians have incorporated into their worldview the notion of salvation through the power of the blood. "Would you be free from the burden of sin? There's power in the blood, power in the blood; would you over evil a victory win? There's wonderful power in the blood. There is power, power, wonder-working power in the blood of the Lamb."[14] Eurochristianity has become obsessed with blood. Not only can pure blood save, as demonstrated by Jesus, but impure blood condemns. A synthesis of faith and politics argues we can be condemned through the possession of impure blood.

The problem with blood is that it can be polluted, thus needing to be cleansed. Before the start of the colonial venture, the concept of *la limpieza de sangre* (the cleansing of the blood) developed in medieval Iberia, an attempt to restore a family's reputation lost through an inter-religious marriage. Focusing on the ancestral line rather than on a conversion of faith, the idea was to "cleanse the blood," specifically Christian blood, from any contamination that resulted by marrying a Jew or a Muslim. The first purity of blood law, passed in Toledo, Spain, in 1449 and approved by the Catholic Church by 1496, required ancestral proof before joining military or religious orders, guilds, government posts, or other organizations. Some of these purity laws lasted four hundred years, into the early twentieth century. The concept of *limpieza de sangre* created two types of people in the world, those with pure blood—Christians—and those with impure blood—non-Christians.

The colonial venture would expand this concept. As conquistadores raped Indian and Black women, a *mestizaje* took hold. Marriage across racial lines was believed to also bring shame to the family and damage their reputation. The metaphysical purity of blood may have originally been religiousized, but now it was racialized. While blood used to be polluted by marrying Jews and Muslims, the concept was expanded to include Indians and Africans. Only white Christians were pure; everyone else—including Christians of color—was genetically and biologically inferior and impure. The only way to *limpia* the blood was to *mejorar la raza* (improve the race) by marrying the whitest person possible, a process known as *blanqueamiento* (whitening) in the Spanish so-called New World. Blood became a metaphysical vehicle toward lineage equality.

This understanding of the impurity of blood was taken to an extreme by Euroamericans. For US whites, unlike their counterparts south of the border, there was no means whatsoever to cleanse blood. They instead developed the legal and social principle of the "one drop rule." One drop was all it took to "pollute" the entire blood. Just one drop of African ancestry makes a person Black regardless of how light their skin pigmentation might be. There is no "*limpieza*" for US Blacks. And here is the problem for Eurochristianity when it comes to blood purity. Because Eurochristianity and whiteness are defined as pure, then all others are impure. There will always be something impure about Black Christians, Native Christians, Latinx Christians, or Asian Christians. They will always be seen as practicing a less pure version of Christianity. We know this to be true because of the invisibility or token representation of minoritized voices in US seminaries and theological schools.

The Problem with Luther

Martin Luther (1483–1546), an Augustinian monk influenced by the *City of God*, even after he left the Catholic Church, argued that God established two kingdoms: the gospel belongs to the kingdom of heaven while law belongs to the kingdom of earth. He erected a barrier between the two by arguing humans must obey earthly civic laws, for without the laws of the state, sin would go unchecked, and chaos would reign. To administer the laws of the state does not require the ruler being a Christian, since laws can still be discerned by reason. And even when such laws are unjust, believers who are not subject to them because they belong to the other kingdom are nevertheless obligated to be obedient, not expecting the state to be governed by the gospel. Such a concept justified some good German Christians who recognized the evils of Nazism to nonetheless be obedient to the law and turn over Jews to the state.

During the Peasant Revolt (1524–25), ironically inspired by Luther's call for liberation, an attempt was made to abolish serfdom. Rather than standing with the disenfranchised seeking their full humanity, Luther made a preferential option for the nobility. He wrote that the only way earthly kingdoms can exist is if there is a certain degree of inequality where some are free and some are not. He wrote:

> You assert that no one is to be the serf of anyone else, because Christ has made us all free . . . Did not Abraham and other patriarchs and prophets have slaves? . . . A slave can be a Christian, and have Christian freedom, in the same way that a prisoner or a sick man is a Christian, and yet be free. [Your claim] would make all men equal, and turn the spiritual kingdom of Christ into

a worldly, external kingdom; and that is impossible.
A worldly kingdom cannot exist without an inequality
of persons, some being free, some imprisoned, some
lords, some subjects.[15]

More damning was his counsel to the authorities as to how
to treat the rebelling serfs. He advised them to "smite, slay,
and stab, secretly or openly, remembering that nothing can
be more poisonous, hurtful, or devilish than a rebel," who
like "mad dogs," must be put down.[16] Political stability for
Luther (and as we will see most Eurochristian thinkers)
takes priority over the oppression of the marginalized.

As problematic as Luther's pronouncements are concerning the support of oppressive political leaders, is his
understanding of grace. He adapted Anselm's satisfaction
theory by emphasizing Jesus's death as a voluntary repay-
ment of debt on behalf of humanity. "Justification by faith"
became foundational within Reformation thinking.[17] Salvation could not be obtained through good works. Salvation
was an unearned gift that when accepted, good works would
naturally flow from the sinner freed from sin's bondage. Experiencing God's forgiveness took precedence over the need
to know the good. God's justice did not mean punishing sinners, but rather, justice or "righteousness" was a free gift
for sinners who lived by faith. We do not become just or

righteous by doing just or righteous deeds, but having been made just and righteous by accepting God's love, we are free to do just and righteous deeds.

The problem with Eurochristianity is how *sola fide* has been interpreted by providing license not to be as concerned about moral or ethical principles. Forgiveness of sin, liberation from guilt, and reconciliation with an angry God through *sola fide* afford the privileged and powerful a sense of impunity, receiving pardon for their sins through Christ without needing to convert from the actions and practices contributing to oppressive social structures, or to provide restitution for all that was immorally taken. South African Archbishop Desmond Tutu reveals the problem with this theology when he says, "If you take my pen and say you are sorry, what good does the apology do me if you still have my pen?" Just accept Jesus as Lord and you will be saved, an acceptance best demonstrated through some verbal confession of sin. Like the days of Merlin, the recital of an incantation—what Eurochristians call a Sinner's Prayer—is supposed to transform the would-be believer into something different than their former self. But like most magic tricks, the illusion of becoming a new creature through a cheap grace that demands nothing simply creates a politically correct religious façade that masks life-denying inner corruption. Amazing grace does not save Eurochristians from sin, but rather saves them to sin. And sin boldly they do.

The Problem with Calvin

John Calvin (1509-1564), more than any other theologian, provided future believers with the groundwork for savage capitalism. Calvin wondered, How do we know we are saved? Like Luther before him, he argued there is nothing humans can do to achieve salvation. There is no act or deed by which one can be saved. God, and God alone, determines each person's eternal fate. There is nothing the chosen can do to be one among God's elect. They cannot rely upon feeling resulting from an emotional conversion experience, for feelings are deceptive. They cannot attempt to do good works, for salvation is a gift, not something that can be earned. They cannot rely on belonging to a particular church, for there are those who attend churches who are among the nonchosen. Election is a sovereign eternal undeserving divine choice that is not based on some divine foreknowledge of how a person's life will unfold, but purely an independent decision made by God according to God's grace and mercy. Humans are either called to eternal life or eternal damnation.

Calvinist thought was abridged through the acronym TULIP—five essential Calvinist doctrines formulated during the second Synod of Dort, some eighty years after his death. Although TULIP is an oversimplification of his message, it has come, nonetheless, to describe his theological contribution to the discourse. "T" stands for the total depravity of humans, making it impossible for humans to save themselves.[18] "U" represents unconditional election, where God unqualifiedly saves certain people, regardless of merit or if deserved.[19] "L" refers to limited atonement, indicating that Christ's sacrifice on the cross was sufficient for saving the elect.[20] "I" means irresistible grace, signifying that who God has chosen will be saved—regardless.[21] And finally, "P" denotes perseverance of the saints, meaning those chosen can never lose their salvation.[22]

If this then is true, if neither an emotional conversion experience, nor good works, nor church membership ensures salvation, how do we know if someone is saved? While only God knows who is elect, there exist signs nonetheless as to who is chosen. One can tell those who are saved, those who are chosen, those who are elect because they are blessed by God.[23] Sociologist Max Weber (1864–1920) was among the first to trace back to Calvin the exchange between a faith encouraging an ethics of abstinence understood as puritanism with economic success, or as he referred to it: "the spirit of capitalism." Spiritualized capitalism flourished in Europe, according to Weber, because it provided the rationale undergirding the religious teachings concerning the "Protestant work ethic." His understanding of Calvinism linked capitalism with Protestantism. If, Weber argued, one knew they were saved by the visible fruits produced by their labor, then attaining social achievements—like wealth—is God's will.

One's labor ceases to be a drudgery, but instead becomes a divine calling. Not only is salvation predestined by God, but also one's occupation. Through one's employment the elect glorify God, and through the blessing incurred by said employment promote the glory of God. Hence there is a moral and divine obligation to work hard as a sign of God's grace. Followers of Calvin's doctrines equated election with financial success, since God blesses the employment of those chosen. One was called to seek wealth ethically and lawfully, and to ignore this calling was to refuse to be a faithful steward of God's blessings.[24]

Think about how most middle-class Eurochristians usually pray. "Thank you, God, for our blessings, our job, our home, our car." Most offer thanksgiving for financial success and possessions. Eurochristian thinking is so rooted in Calvinist thought that we still, to this day, equate economic success with being chosen by God. But if wealth indicates God's calling, then what is the flip side of that coin? Is poverty a sign of God's rejection? Eurochristianity seems to believe so—hence the missionary activities seeking conversion of the indigent before ministering to their physical needs. The houseless are on the streets because they lack a trust in God. If they can be saved, then their predicament would resolve itself as God would open the floodgates of heaven and shower new blessings upon the newly converted. And because people of color are disproportionately poor in the

United States, it seems to justify that God loves and chooses whiteness over and against them.

The problem with Calvin is that if Euroamericans determine who is elected by God based on their bank statement, then people like Donald Trump are, as many Evangelicals believe, God's anointed. But what if poverty has nothing to do with God's rejection? What if poverty is the consequence of an unequal distribution of resources? If this is true, then those seen as financially "blessed" really do not have a right to their riches. Their wealth is not a blessing from God for their faithfulness in glorifying God through their labor. Instead, the poverty of others is directly connected to the riches of those who are "blessed," not by God, but by their living within social structures that often bless them due to whiteness. What Calvinism accomplished is the justification and legitimization of the exploitation of workers by mislabeling capitalist business drive for profit as a calling from God, extinguishing any passion for social justice by the frozen chosen.

The Problem with Salvation History

History has an end, and that end is Jesus, specifically his return and the establishment of God's kingdom. Salvation history argues that humanity is moving through time toward an ultimate end where all who are called will find their eternal rest. This abstract theological and historical trajectory became, in the Eurocentric imagination, a spiritual justification for atrocities against those not deemed "saved." When the original thirteen colonies gazed westward with an avaricious hunger for land, they needed a divine mandate that justified land theft and genocide as the will of God. "Our manifest destiny," John O'Sullivan, editor of the *Democratic Review*, wrote, is "to overspread the continent allotted by Providence for the free development of our yearly multiplying millions."[25] Just as the Israelites were given the Promised Land, so too were Euroamericans as the new Israel. The Almighty's final solution for the original inhabitants of the land who stood in the way of possession was genocide, whether they be Canaanites,[26] Cheyenne, or Comanches. For Euroamericans, adhering to a postmillennialist theology, Christ's second coming after a thousand years of peace on earth that would usher in the establishment of God's kingdom would come to pass once the apocalyptic mission of conquering the new "Promised Land" was fully realized.[27]

Missouri Senator Thomas Hart Benton (1821–1851) articulated this divine mission of the "white" race being faithful to its "divine command to subdue and replenish the earth," by destroying "savagery," and replacing the "wigwam" with the "Capitol," the "savage" with the "Christian," and the "red squaws" with the "white matrons."[28] Josiah Strong, an influential minister and a leader of the liberal social gospel movement saw in 1885 land theft and genocide as the means of bringing the saving message of Jesus to the entire world: "It seems to me that God, with infinite wisdom and skill, is training the Anglo-Saxon race for an hour sure to come in the world's future. . . . If I read not amiss, this powerful race will move down upon Mexico, down upon Central and South America, out upon the islands of the sea, over upon Africa and beyond. And can any one doubt that the result of this competition of races will be the 'survival of the fittest'?"[29]

The conquest of nonwhites is not an evil, but a Christianizing and civilizing benefit for so-called savages. Consider the 1837 words of Senator John C. Calhoun of South Carolina given on the Senate floor arguing that slavery was not an evil but a good for both races: "But let me not be understood as admitting, even by implication, that the existing relations between the two races in slaveholding states is an evil:—far otherwise; I hold it to be a good, as it has thus far proved itself to be to both, and will continue to prove so if not disturbed by the fell spirit of abolition. I appeal to facts. Never before has the black race of Central Africa, from the dawn of history to the present day, attained a condition so civilized and so improved, not only physically, but morally and intellectually. It came among us in a low, degraded, and savage condition, and in the course of a few generations it has grown up under the fostering care of our institutions . . .

to its present comparatively civilized condition . . . conclusive proof of the general happiness of the race."[30]

The problem with US salvation history is that this divine mission of Euroamericans can only occur with the decimation of nonwhites who stand in their way while simultaneously defining such decimation as a blessing for those being slaughtered. Benevolent violence has historically been how the will of Euroamericans, understood as the will of God, has been enforced. Ensuring white supremacy became the impetus for the genocide of the original people of the land, slavery, Jim and Jane Crow, Gunboat Diplomacy, the establishment of Banana Republics, and when they did not get their way after a fair and secure election—the storming of the Capitol to overturn the will of the people.

The Problem with Rauschenbusch

Walter Rauschenbusch (1861–1918), a proponent of the social gospel movement that was a response to the extreme unchecked capitalism of his time, is usually praised by liberal Eurochristians for his move away from the normative pietism toward an embrace of justice-based socialist movements. Christians are to respond to the deep-rooted sinfulness of the social order by working for God's kingdom of justice. No doubt his views resonate with those seeking a more gospel-centered message. He argued that "we learn from the gospels, for instance, that God is on the side of the poor, and that he proposes to view anything done or not done to them as having been done or not done to him. Such a revelation of solidarity and humanity comes with a regenerating shock to our selfish minds."[31] But regardless of how much this message might resonate with those on the margins of US society, he nonetheless was an advocate for white supremacy, arguing for "the social supremacy of the Aryan race."[32] White supremacy, and the unearned power, profit, and privilege it assures is God ordained: "It is Providential that Teutons hold the largest part of the world's wealth and power in the hollow of their hands, and the larger share of the world's intellectual and spiritual possessions in the hollow of their heads. They are a princely stock, these fair skinned men, an imperial race, as they stand at the forge of time and hammer out history."[33] For him, "Jesus is on the side of America."[34]

Ethnic superiority was not an excuse to lord it over those falling short of whiteness, but rather to express paternalistic concern about "the problem of the black man." As Jim and Jane Crow took hold throughout Southern states, he proposed that the solution would be the transformation of Blacks through the example provided to them by middle-class whites. For him "the Christian way out is to take our belated black brother by the hand and urge him along the road of steady and intelligent labor, of property rights, of family fidelity, of hope and self-confidence, and of pride and joy in his race achievement."[35] Besides voicing concern about the problem with Blacks, he also expressed concern with the "cheap and docile" immigrants "burden[ing American] cities with an undigested mass of alien people" who "checked the propagation of the Teutonic stock."[36] He expressed apprehension over miscegenation, warning of the danger of Teutonic blood mixing with Slav, Spanish, or "negro" blood, asking: "Can the racial characteristics of the Teutons hold their predominance against this blending of stock?"[37]

Rauschenbusch's white supremacy went hand-in-hand with the Manifest Destiny that advocated global dominance. During a sermon given shortly after the conclusion of the Spanish-American War, the war that launched the United States into the colonial race for possession of other nations' economies, he preached: "There is in the heart of our people a deep sense of destiny, of a mission laid upon us by the Ruler of history . . . [God] has made clear his will by the irrepressible force of events. We shall have to accept and obey."[38] Empire becomes a tool in the hands of God by which Christians can be protected from the hatred of nonbelievers. "[St.] Paul," Rauschenbusch writes, "certainly did not regard the Empire as Satanic in character, but as a divine instrument of order and justice, a power holding the anti-Christian malignity in check."[39]

The problem with Rauschenbusch is that he provides Euroamericans justification for seeing the United States as an empire called into being by God. The Empire and the Christian faith for him were born "simultaneously" during the reign of Augustus. They were, as he states, "twins by birth." Therefore, they ought to be "in helpful relations to each other in accordance with the manifest purpose of God." Christians, he argues, possess "the highest morality," hence they are the ones called to secure the Empire. "As the soul holds the body together," he explains, "so Christians hold the world together."[40] Eurochristian churches were being called by God to fulfill their imperialist calling, a Manifest Destiny that they do not seek but have an obligation to fulfill.

The Problem with Niebuhr

Reinhold Niebuhr (1892–1971), although in his youth a socialist, called later in life for an imperial ethics that became influential among conservatives and supposed liberals. During a *New York Times* interview, then-presidential candidate Barack Obama referenced Niebuhr by stating, "I love him. He's one of my favorite philosophers." Obama went on to say: "I take away the compelling idea that there's serious evil in the world, and hardship and pain. And we should be humble and modest in our belief we can eliminate those things. But we shouldn't use that as an excuse for cynicism and inaction. I take away . . . swinging from naïve idealism to bitter realism."[41]

If Rauschenbusch became the patron saint of today's liberals, Niebuhr can be considered the patron saint of neoconservatives. He moved the discourse away from the social optimism of the early twentieth century toward what he called a Christian realism, prominent during the mid-century. But because he approached reality through a Eurocentric lens, he fell short of critical engagement with his—and the public's—unexamined white supremacy. An apologist for the role of the United States in a so-called free world, he justified the injustices associated with empire for the sake of Cold-War expedience. After years of Nazism, and with the emergence of a "godless" Soviet Union, he believed the United States had a moral obligation to assume world leadership. Anglo-Saxons had a God-ordained responsibility to take on the global leadership role.[42] In other words, the premier ethicist of the time claimed God destined Eurochristians to lead the world. While the nineteenth-century Manifest Destiny was continental, Niebuhr's twentieth-century call was global! Anglo-Saxon imperialism was a preferable alternative to Nazism, and later Communism. Fearing the global anarchy that resulted with the closure of the Second World War, he called for "realistic imperialistic" Anglo-Saxons.[43] The need for a stable world in an age of nuclear armament led Niebuhr to prioritize order over certain inequalities.

Yes, the danger existed that the United States could overreach, but for Niebuhr, ethics was understood as minimizing (not eliminating) injustices. Both Niebuhr's and Obama's realism understood that for the United States to assume a global leadership, order within the global arena (and within domestic society) is required. If we desire society to properly function, then certain injustices and inequalities become necessary. As he explained, "No complex society will be able to dispense with certain inequalities of privilege. Some of them are necessary for the proper performance of certain social functions; and others (though this is not so certain) may be needed to prompt energy and diligence in the performance of important functions."[44] Most Eurochristian thinkers, like Niebuhr, are sympatico with calls for justice, as long as society's necessary equilibrium is not threatened. Hence in the name of the law and order advocated by Eurochristian nationalists, justice is sacrificed on the altar of expedience.

Love, according to Niebuhr, may be the ideal Christian virtue, but it remains an impractical basis for public action, falling short of the complexities of modern society. Subscribing to a forced dualism of previous thinkers, Niebuhr continues in the tradition of Augustine's "two cities," thirteenth-century canonists' "two luminaries," or Martin Luther's "two kingdoms." A dichotomy continues to be foundational for Eurochristianity between the "private" and "public," where the "private" places the individual under the dictates of God while the "public" excuses the injustices of whatever powers and principalities happen to be ruling. Humans are called to individualist moral behavior. Multinational corporations and nations, unlike humans, are simply incapable of such behavior. Niebuhr justifies the necessity of injustices in the name of social order.

Niebuhr's realism became an ideological apologetics of the global dominance of the United States. We see this neo-conservative move made for Eurochristian nationalism in Niebuhr's book written during the close of his prolific career, *The Structure of Nations and Empires*. Accepting the reality of the recurring phenomena of the inevitability of empires, Niebuhr sets out to garner historical lessons that the United States can implement as a check against what he perceived to be the global aggressive designs of the Soviet Union. Colonialism is not presented as a moral evil, but an ambiguous necessity where humanity could benefit from the "tutelage of colonialism." As a neutral force, colonialism—when done correctly—can be a positive force to lift countries like China or India that were "on the primitive level of tribal life."[45]

Consequently, empire is not in itself immoral when used as trustees for civilization that "bestow a value of universal validity." The United States had a moral obligation to become—through empire—"servant to the universal community." And in an unbelievable lack of self-awareness, Niebuhr argues

Explain (handwritten note in top margin)

the United States should impose moral dominance because of their moral superiority: "[The US] moral advantage lies in the fact that [it] does not have a strong lust for power which always accompanies its possession." For him, the power possessed by the United States "need not be expressed in military terms . . . The desire to expand the superior culture is one of the motives of imperial expansion."[46]

In the final analysis, the problem with Niebuhr is merging neoconservatism with white supremacy, a self-understanding adopted by liberals—even those who are not physically white. Obama channeling Niebuhr is not that different from how it was manifested by Trump. While Trump dismisses primitive people coming from "shithole countries,"[47] presidents like Obama or Biden demonstrate greater tact, but nonetheless remain as complicit with Niebuhr's neoconservatism. What Obama, Trump, and Biden have in common is that all three are ontologically white males. To be the leader of the empire, it matters not if you are Black or white, male or female. All presidents—past and future—can serve only if they are fully committed to everything Euromaleness symbolizes within global dominance. Even indigenous Secretary of the Interior Deb Haaland or biracial bi-ethnic Vice President Kamala Harris of the Biden Administration are ontologically white males. Regardless of the race or gender of whoever gets to sit in the oval office, the titans of industry can never be threatened by national or international politics. If such a threat was to arise, the full forces at the disposal of the president would be unleashed to maintain the current economic power structures even at the expense of communities of color that might share the same skin pigmentation or gender as the president.

The emperor or empress has a global responsibility to secure the interest of the empire—whatever the cost. It matters less if an ontologically white male sees other countries as shithole nations or in need of paternalistic leadership. If required, troops will be sent to any corner of the world to protect the interests of McDonald's, Microsoft, or Mobil. Presidents are chosen based on who best sustains the privilege of a Eurochristian nation comprised of 4.3 percent of the global population[48] yet consuming 20 percent of the world's energy[49]—an imbalance that must be maintained through military force if need be. In such a world, it makes little difference what the race, gender, or ethnicity of the commander-in-chief is. The electoral decision for those calling themselves progressive is really choosing who would do less global damage, not who will stand with the wretched of the earth. From electoral cycle to electoral cycle, an illusion of democracy is maintained, masking the realism that regardless of who gets elected, the country's distribution of opportunities and income will continue to be determined based on ethnicity and race as each presidential term ends with a greater wealth gap than when it began.

CHAPTER 3

The Problem with Hauerwas

Probably no current Eurocentric thinker has been more influential in reinforcing Eurochristianity than Stanley Hauerwas (1940-). Affectionally called "Stan the man" by his devotees, he is—in the full sense of the word—the Man, credited for renewing the central role of the church in ethical thought. While Hauerwas, and all the other contributors to Eurochristianity before him, may not necessarily hold racist thoughts or biases, they nevertheless aided and abetted racism by constructing a Christianity reflecting white supremacy. Hauerwas contributes to this trajectory by guiding Eurochristians toward a way of being that allows white supremacy to continue operating at top efficiency regardless of the rhetoric to the contrary. White supremacy works best when it focuses on virtues, when it attempts to define virtues without any obligation whatsoever to implement said virtues for the purpose of bringing about social change. Hauerwasian thought advocates a faith devoid of praxis, a belief, which like a deadly virus, has infected the whole Eurocentric church.

For Hauerwas, the task of the gathering of believers "is not to *make* the world the kingdom, but to be faithful to the kingdom by showing to the world what it means to be a community of peace."[50] To be a Eurochristian has everything to do with being the church, not living out one's duty or responsibility to the gospel. He argues: "the current emphasis on justice and rights as the primary norms guiding the social witness of Christians is in fact a mistake."[51] He insists that "the first task of Christian social ethics, therefore, is not to make the 'world' better or more just, but to help Christian people form their community consistent with their conviction that the story of Christ is a truthful account of our existence."[52] Therefore, "the church and Christians must be uninvolved in the polity of our society and involved in the polity that is the church."[53]

For Eurocentric thinkers like Hauerwas, seeking to establish social justice is more a response to the Enlightenment project than to the gospel, and thus should be rejected. Eurochristians are called to be the church bound together not by what they do to the least of these (what he calls a gesture), but by how they create community, remaining distant from "progressive forces," as well as "political change and justice."[54] Hence, while remaining cognizant of being a "white southerner from the lower-middle classes who grew up embedded in the practices of segregation" who does not fully grasp how the "habits of racism" continue to influence him, he nevertheless dismisses the cry for justice emanating from the underside of his whiteness by dismissing the experience of the racially oppressed as not being his experience. Hauerwas argues that "to 'use' Martin Luther King Jr., and the church that made him possible, to advance my understanding of 'Christian ethics' seems wrong. That is not *my* story, though I pray that God will make that story my story, for I hope to enjoy the fellowship of the communion of the saints. Yet that is an eschatological hope, which, as much as one desires it, cannot be forced."[55] How convenient for him to ignore the reality of the Black experience that *is* the other side of the same American coin of the white supremacy to which he was a beneficiary.

Correct doctrine (codeword for Eurocentric doctrine) is more important than correct action. The focus is not on the doing, but in the thinking of the doing, or as he explains: "what kind of agents they think themselves to be in doing what they do."[56] Like all other Eurocentric thinkers, Hauerwas confuses Christianity with a Eurocentric interpretation of Christianity, an interpretation that masks and justifies whites' dominance in the theological discourse as well as the overall culture. Making a preferential option for the white church, Hauerwas argues that "the primary social task of the church is to be itself,"[57] a terrifying proposition for those who have lived on the underside of Eurochristian churches that historically sanctioned genocide, colonialism, and the oppression of the Global South.

The problem with Hauerwas is that he provided a moral option for many liberal and conservative Eurochristian churches in the late twentieth century to celebrate a do-nothing ethics, an exclusive church that resembles a country club rather than a place where believers gather to live out the calling of the gospel. The Eurochristian church Hauerwas envisioned is a sectarian one for Euroamericans who have no desire to establish justice. Should we therefore be surprised he has become so popular among Eurochristians? By reinforcing the unexamined white supremacy of the dominant culture's churches, Hauerwas has provided Eurochristians with ecclesiastical cover. He may insist "there is no ideal church, no mystically existing church more real than the concrete church of parking lots and potluck dinners,"[58] but such a church has little resemblance to the calling of the gospel. But on that day, they will come before me saying: "Lord, Lord, did we not pave church parking lots in your name, and did we not hold pot-luck dinners for you?" But I will respond, "Away from me, you evildoers, for I never knew you." For that which was not done (praxis) to the least of these, was not done unto me.

Why Bother?

During a November 13, 2021, "ReAwaken America Tour," conservatives gathered at Reverend John Hagee's San Antonio Cornerstone church to hear Michael Flynn, Trump's former National Security advisor. Flynn proclaimed, "If we are going to have one nation under God, which we must, we have to have one religion. One nation under God, and one religion under God."[59] Ironically, this is the same person who spent years peddling the conspiracy theory, throughout numerous speeches, that Democrats sought to implement Islamic Shariah law.[60] The concern for Flynn is not the creation of a theocracy, but the creation of a theocracy that is not Eurochristian. *Ein reich, ein volk, ein gott!* Proving that being a Eurochristian has nothing to do with a person's faith or belief tradition, a GOP Ohio Senate candidate—who is Jewish (or a Jewish Eurochristian)—tweeted "We Stand with General Flynn"[61] in response to the backlash that ensued. And while Euroamericans move to privilege Eurochristianity at the expense of other faith traditions, doctors of the church spend their energies instead seeking to find some new tidbit about some dead theologian—predominately a dead white theologian who is incapable of providing a word for today's marginalized. No wonder the voices emerging from Eurochristianity have become morally irrelevant to the body politic as more and more people abandon the church, caring less about what it has to say.

Eurochristianity is—and has always been—a rejection of the message proclaimed by the Jesus presented in the Gospels; it is the lap dog of antichrists. The mere fact it has been used as a justification for crusades, inquisition, colonialization, and slavery clearly demonstrates its sulfuric roots. While the message of the gospel advances the theological proposition that we are all created in the image of God (*imago Dei*), Eurochristianity instead has advocated the divine right to steal the land and bodies of others. While Jesus taught the principle of loving one's neighbor by placing their needs first, Eurochristian nationalism has insisted on the power and privilege due to those chosen by God. This leaves those relegated to the underside of this Eurochristian nationalism, specifically those hailing from communities of color, asking if Christianity is so beyond reform that no version or manifestation can ever truly be salvific.

Eurochristianity is, after all, a death-dealing ideology that has choked the spirit out of the message of Jesus Christ. If we pay close attention, we can hear Jesus gasping for air, crying out "I can't breathe!" We who have suffered under the yoke of Eurochristianity must ask if its ways that developed over the past two millennia are detrimental to the well-being of all who do not possess white skin and life-denying to those living on the margins of white supremacy by providing the justification for a political apartheid structure designed to erase the voices of communities of color. If so, why then embrace the oppressor's faith tradition? For a person of color to bow their knees before a white Jesus is to become complicit with and to contribute to their own oppression. The racially, ethnically, and sexually disenfranchised who choose to worship in churches that praise the religious ideology justifying their oppression betray their community's cry for liberation. Rejecting Eurochristianity is not a rhetorical slogan; it is a call to action with eyes wide open as to how this faith tradition practiced by Euroamericans is detrimental to communities of color. We are left wondering if Jesus can be saved from Eurochristianity. If there is no hope, then we must hasten Eurochristianity's demise. For our very survival, for our very salvation, let us come together and dig the graves of Eurochristian nationalism and bury, once and for all, this scourge of humanity.

4

Celebrating Ignorance

To embrace a geocentric, flat-earth worldview, despite satellite images, is a matter of pure stupidity. This is not a contrary view worthy of consideration in the matrix of public opinion—it is an indicator of ignorance. Employing the overwhelming abundance of science and rational thought to demonstrate how ludicrous this position is does not make one an academic elitist. And yet, while education can cure society from ridiculous propositions like the flat-earth conspiracy theory, a crusade to delegitimize education has been championed from Tucker to Trump.

Unfortunately, there exists no eloquent or polite way of saying someone is plain stupid. To reject the findings of immunologists, climatologists, or sociologists in favor of ideological quackery that neatly fits into one's fantasy worldview is the trait of an ignoramus. And yet, intelligence is ridiculed. Ignorance is embraced not for ignorance's sake, but usually because it panders to white rage. Anger and ignorance are powerful political tools. If Euroamericans are angry and ignorant enough, then they can serve the interests of those who can manipulate their anger and ignorance for profit. For example, climate change denial benefits the petroleum industry, the Big Lie of massive voter fraud benefits Republicans unable to get elected due to demographic shifts, evolution denial benefits Eurochristian fundamentalism, fear of socialism benefits the billionaire class through lower taxes, and hostility toward critical race theory benefits white supremacy.

This is not to argue that those with PhDs after their names know the answers. While ignorance facilitates oppressive horrors, education at times is complicit. Education can either be conditioned for domestication by, or liberation from, the existing social structures. All too often, the educational system serves to normalize authoritarian power structures as legitimate. True—education provides the possibility of raising consciousness. But all too often, the unexamined embrace of white supremacy by those with PhDs remains, nonetheless, privileged by structures of oppression.

Any scientist or academic worth their degree would argue that a healthy hermeneutical suspicion should challenge the arena in which power, all too often, creates knowledge. What is defined as truth often becomes the self-serving opinions of those who hold the power to dictate reality.

But, when the scientific method is employed, when peer reviewers examine the data, when the voices of those from the margins of the scientific community are taken into consideration, then what is being presented as a possible truth has greater weight than *comemierdas* who base their faith on QAnon conspirators. An education that liberates lifts consciousness by demonstrating how to see with one's own eyes while one's feet remain firmly planted within one's social location. This explains why intellectuals are perceived as dangerous by wannabe authoritarians. The goal is to domesticate the masses by making them asses, and conspiracy theories become the means by which to achieve said goal. Such a strategy calls for the decimation of intellectuals committed to raise the consciousness of those smoking the opiate of white supremacy and those impacted by its fumes.

Conspiracy theories have always existed within political discourses; however, they have usually been relegated to the fringes—until recently. They began to make themselves more mainstream with the rise of figures like vice-presidential hopeful Sarah Palin who insisted on the existence of "death panels" during the Obamacare debate. Palin, and others who sold the public on the lie of death panels, knew none existed, but the lie served the purpose of gravitating a populace who were frightened into believing the absurd. The Orwellian falsehood contributed to the formation of the Tea Party that accepted as truth government conspiracies within a milieu ripe for authoritarians willing to supplant truths with lies. To insist on truth becomes an inconvenience stunting the lie's effectiveness. Consider Trump's advocacy for the conspiracy theory that Obama was born in Kenya. If the lie can lead to a greater and unearned share of privilege, profit, and power, then it behooves those who know better to believe the lie.

The Purpose for Lying

For Trumpism to triumph, an ignorant Euroamerican electorate is required. Eurochristianity must become a faith that fosters, supports, and celebrates ignorance. Outlandish lies and buffoonery acts are designed to numb the public—like opioids—from the challenges raised from fact-finding and truth-telling. The brains of Eurochristian nationalists are so devoured by lies and conspiracy theories that their bodies become easier to manipulate and control. Political authoritarianism begins with a lie, the more outrageous, the better. One such lie advanced by Trump is that the 2020 election was rigged and stolen, the greatest fraud ever perpetrated upon the American public. Although Trump's own Department of Homeland Security issued a statement stating that "the November 3rd election was the most secure in American history,"[1] Trump nevertheless engaged in a preposterous lie. Regardless of hard evidence to the contrary, the lie was believed because it titillated the half-eaten minds of ignora-muses, propelling many to storm the nation's Capitol in the name of the lie. The lie of a stolen election is crucial for the important purpose it serves—the delegitimization of truth. Such a lie is designed to undermine elected authority, keeping hatred simmering while maintaining the father of lies in the political spotlight.

The Big Lie of a stolen election did not begin in 2020 when Trump lost to Biden. Roger Stone, notorious self-described "dirty trickster," set up the "Stop the Steal" website in 2016 to raise funds and rally the troops in the event Trump would lose to Clinton. Let's not forget that Trump, when he lost the Iowa caucus to Ted Cruz (R-TX), accused the senator of tampering with the election results. When it appeared he might be denied the 2016 primary nomination, he claimed a "Bush-Cruz-Kasich-Romney-Ryan-McConnell faction" were in cahoots to steal the nomination. When it seemed like he might lose to Hillary Clinton, he stated she could only win through election fraud. The loss of the House during the midterm election was also interpreted as voter fraud.[2] And like the boy who cried wolf once too many times, he blamed his 2020 defeat on—you guessed it—election tampering. Two days after the election, as votes were still being tallied, Trump's eldest son, Don Jr., was texting then-White House chief of staff Mark Meadows on how to subvert the election.[3]

Stop the Steal was not some grassroots movement. It was a sophisticated four-year coordinated political operation that perpetuated a lie that incited an insurrection on January 6th. We all know it is a Big Lie because sixty failed legal suits claiming fraud were found lacking by judges, many of whom were appointed by Trump. We all know it is a Big Lie because Republican-controlled state legislatures refused White House pressure to not certify the election. We all know it is a Big Lie because as Trump's lawyers were claiming Dominion voting machines conspired with George Soros and Venezuela to switch Trump votes to Biden, an internal memo from the Trump election team concluded these allegations were untrue.[4] Even Attorney General William Barr of Trump's Justice Department said on December 1, 2020, that the election was untainted by significant fraud and that Mr. Biden was the legitimate winner of the election. And while we celebrate those from the president's own political party who at great personal cost sacrificed future political ambitions to defend the ideals of democracy, there were others who, knowing that election fraud did not occur, chose to nevertheless drink the Trump Kool-Aid. Their refusal to speak truth in the midst of falsehood has led to 36 percent of the public—over a third of the population—to believe, a year later, that Biden did not win the election. Among Republicans, 78 percent believe Biden lost, and 54 percent believe solid evidence exists that proves Biden's loss.[5] Of course, no such evidence exists, and no such evidence has ever been presented. Truth is reimagined because politicians who know what is true find the lie politically more useful.

Whenever those who have historically been politically marginalized play by the rules and gain voice, the most Euroamerican thing to do is to suppress their voices. The lie serves a greater purpose than simply pacifying the bruised ego of an election loser; it provides the means by which to politically silence those who were never supposed to have had a voice in this country. Questioning the integrity of the election riles up the base and provides an excuse for Republican-controlled state legislatures to enact voter-suppression laws. Of course, few politicians actually believe the lie. But if the lie is maintained, justification for changing election laws to silence communities of color can be accomplished.

It would of course be difficult to advance anti-democratic legislation under the banner of "suppressing the votes of people of color." Enacting laws that undermine the democratic will of the people is a difficult proposition to sell. More effective is to spin a lie concerning voting integrity. Much easier to claim a need to protect the integrity of the voting system by perpetuating the lie of voter fraud; thus, a campaign is designed to deal with a problem that does not exist. Who could argue with the noble task of safeguarding democracy even though such high-sounding rhetoric masks the real goal of strengthening apartheid? Voter integrity becomes code language for voter suppression.

The lie is also profitable. And while it is true that politicians throughout the ages have engaged in hyperbole, what we are currently witnessing is something more disturbing and threatening. Disinformation, as a way of being, is utilized to scare the ignorant into giving money and voting against their own self-interest. Consider the eight or so Republican congresspersons who sent fundraising emails claiming President Biden was giving every undocumented immigrant $450,000. One of those lawmakers, Senator John Kennedy (R-LA), included a link labeled: "RUSH $500 TO STOP ILLEGAL PAYMENTS!" The solicitation email went on to claim, "I'm watching Joe Biden pay illegals to come into our country, and it's all being paid for by raising YOUR taxes." Or consider the email of Representative Jake LaTurner (R-KS) who, among other things, wrote, "Parents are simply protesting a radical curriculum in public schools, and Biden wants the parents labeled terrorists. Will you consider donating now to help us fight back against this disgusting abuse of power?"[6]

Finally, the lie is crucial in maintaining the justification for white supremacy. Look again at the top two fund solicitation emails and how they are racist dog whistles. The first scares Euroamericans into giving to stop the Brown "illegals" from being lured into this country with almost a half million-dollar incentive, while the second email scares Euroamericans with the imposition of critical race theory. Although spouting white supremacist rhetoric was once enough to motivate the Euroamerican masses to support politicians who curtail the participation of those who fell short of whiteness, today such blatant racism is considered by many nauseating, even among blatant racists. Instead of arguing we need to suppress the votes of nonwhites, the lie of rigged elections becomes more politically correct, providing rhetorical cover for those committed to white supremacy. The Big Lie justifies rigging future electoral processes in the noble attempt to maintain the integrity of voting. Fighting against imaginary election rigging safeguards the implementation of election rigging.

Birds Aren't Real

How does one prove that which does not exist? Those claiming there is a Santa Claus need not provide evidence of his existence; the burden of proof falls upon those who know he is but a figment of the imagination. Critical thinking is thus turned on its head when the evidence-based truth is not only reduced to an opinion, but those perpetuating the lie demand their lie must be proven wrong while dismissing every and all empirical evidence as fake. How does one prove the earth is not flat when NASA satellite images are dismissed as a hoax? Or that the moon landing was staged in a studio? To simply claim the election was stolen, even while all governmental investigations mostly led by Republican officials and certified by Republican state legislators prove the opposite, is not enough. Anecdotes, not proof; innuendoes, not statistical probabilities—these are the tools employed by those who suspend reality for the sake of ideology. And yet, the argument that the election was not stolen requires proof from those who base their conclusion upon hard scientific facts, facts dismissed as subjective and tainted by perpetrators of the lie. The purpose of the lie is not to prove what the perpetrator of the lie thinks occurred; the lie exists for the sole purpose of introducing doubt to reality.

Embracing the lie of a rigged election is preferable even when the overwhelming evidence proves this assertion to be an obvious lie spun to empower Euroamericans fearful of losing their white-privileged status within society. Based on this lie, Arizona Republicans ordered a partisan investigation of the ballots cast in Maricopa County to prove Trump and not Biden won. Not surprisingly, the recount showed Trump lost by a larger margin than reported on election night.[7] One would think that the expensive Republican-led audit would cause people to pause and return to their senses. Once the Big Lie was proven in Arizona to be just that—a lie—believers continued to suspend reality. They launched another sham audit in Texas as other states moved to follow suit.

Not surprisingly, the celebration of ignorance for political manipulation also leads to the full-throttle embrace of the lunacy of conspiracy theories. Take for example the hundreds who travelled from all over the United States to gather on November 2, 2021, at the grassy knoll of Dealey Plaza in downtown Dallas wearing "Trump-Kennedy 2024" shirts. They came expecting the reappearance of John F. Kennedy Jr., who they believe didn't die in 1999 and is Q himself. Supposedly the son of the former president would appear on the anniversary of his father's assassination to become Trump's running mate. The second coming of Kennedy would trigger the permanent return of Trump to power.[8] They came to Dallas because this prediction was issued by Q.

No greater proof exists that we are living in a post-truth nihilistic America than the rise of QAnon. For Q so loved the world that he gave us his only beloved son, Trump, that whosoever believeth in him shall not perish during the Storm but have life. Q—like God—is all knowing and all seeing, guiding the faithful in a world whose domain belongs to Satan and his disciples. The term Q comes from a government clearance designation that provides access to top secret restrictive data; hence the belief that Q is a high-level official within the Trump administration with access to classified information. "Anon" stands for anonymous. The QAnon phenomenon dates to October 2017 when the first post attributed to Q was published on an anonymous account called Q Clearance Patriot. Early followers of Q originally believed that Trump was engaged in a war against a cabal who controlled the government and media. On the Day of Judgement, the apocalyptic day of the Storm, Trump's second coming will take place. He will return to rule over the earth and judge the wicked, ushering in a golden age. By August 2018, Q signs began to appear at Trump re-election rallies.

Who are the wicked within a Q worldview? Liberals who are part of a global cabal of Satan worshippers who sought to overthrow the Trump presidency while participating in the literal raping and eating of babies. These murderous pedophiles include luminaries like Barack Obama, Hillary Clinton, George Soros, Tom Hanks, Anderson Cooper, Pope Francis, and the Rothschilds family, just to name a few. They control governments, media, Hollywood, and of course, global banking institutions. Trump knows of this cabal and was chosen by God to bring an end to these evildoers. On the Day of the Storm, a messianic Trump will return, leading the military in a brutal takeover of the country. The demonic hedge that surrounds and protects Biden will, on that day, be uprooted. Thousands of nefarious liberal pedophiles will be arrested and sent to Guantanamo Bay prison to face military tribunals where they will be tried and executed. Once Trump sits on the throne, and all evil liberals have been banished for all eternity, the faithful will enter their salvation as humanity gets to live in a new earth, a perfect union prepared for the faithful since the foundation of the earth.

Trump (referred to as Q+) and his officials, during his presidency, validated and amplified QAnon by consistently retweeting conspiracies generated from Q-affiliated accounts, referred to as Qdrops.[9] But Trump lost, and the Storm did not materialize. One would think this would bring an end to Q; however, ignorance is durable, leading to death and destruction, as demonstrated during the Capitol insurrection where Q followers participated in the storming of Congress in hopes of igniting the Storm prophesied by Q. Known as "accelerationists," they believe in hastening the timeline of the coming apocalypse by taking radical actions that will bring forth the inevitable collapse of democracy, ideally through the instigation of a coup that would force Trump's hand to take over the government. January 6th was not supposed to end with the certification of Biden's electoral win but be the beginning of the Q utopia. Obviously, belief in Q is based on faith, not facts. The goal is not to prove the obvious, that QAnon is a LARP (Live-Action Role Play). To engage in a reason-based argument to repudiate ignorance only confirms in the ignoramus's mind that the one seeking to raise consciousness is the true fool.

While similar conspiracies have always been a staple of American democracy, they mostly were relegated to the fringes of society. What is different with QAnon is how rapidly it moved to a centralized belief in both the Republican Party and Eurochristianity. Almost a quarter of Republicans (23%) believe in QAnon conspiracies, while almost 26 percent of white evangelicals, 22 percent of Mormons, 25 percent of Black Protestants, 24 percent of Protestants of color, 19 percent of white Catholics, 18 percent of white Protestants, 17 percent of non-Christians, 29 percent of Hispanic Protestants, and 27 percent of Hispanic Catholics (*ay, Dios mio*) believe the Storm is coming (the lowest supporters of QAnon are Jews at 2 percent). Revolutions and government overthrows have historically taken place with less supporters. Just as frightening, about one in five of all Americans believe things have gotten so far off track that true American patriots may have to resort to violence to save America, with about a third of Republicans and over a quarter of white evangelicals believing in violence as a justifiable alternative. [10]

Here is the irony: Eurochristians—regardless of race, ethnicity, or faith tradition—believe in a QAnon crusade against the sexual abuse of what is claimed to be 800,000 children, even though not a single child's bones have ever been discovered to substantiate this claim. They stand against evil by following Q's pronouncements that appeared on 4chan (later 8chan and now 8kun), an imageboard hosting site comprising user-created message boards, a site that has also attracted and posted child pornographers, hate groups, and hate-based mass shooting manifestos (Christchurch *why should we believe this?*

Mosque, Poway Synagogue, El Paso shooting). The QAnon fight against a liberal cannibal pedophobia cabal is hosted on a site that created discussion threads on child rape and where explicit child pornography was shared. Such incongruencies would be laughable if not for the increasing body count caused by the claims pulled out of 8kun's derrière.

Also ironic is how foreign powers weaponized Q, turning so-called patriots into traitors against their own government, even to the point of seeking to violently overturn election results. According to US intelligence services, Russia, Iran, Saudi Arabia, and China heightened US discontent and discord by utilizing Q disinformation to compromise legitimate political processes, radicalize Q believers, and incite violence. These "patriots," believing the absurd, like the second coming of John-John, become tools for adversary countries to undermine the US government.[11] But foreign countries are not the sole threat. America is being torn apart by ignorance from within. Almost forty candidates for national office during the 2022 midterm elections have publicly stated their support for QAnon and its conspiracy theories.[12]

White supremacy rooted in QAnon conspiracies make victims out of its defenders as they transform into uncivilized and savage beings. Support of white privilege requires a dehumanization that engenders brutish behavior. To accomplish this task, QAnon reaches into its anti-Semitic bag of hatred. The belief that liberals are kidnapping children for the purpose of rape and cannibalism is but a modern incarnation of the anti-Semitic tropes dating to medieval times when Jews supposedly kidnapped Christian children and used their blood to make matzah. Voicing such false accusations gave rise to righteous indignation, leading the so-called faithful to visit upon the Jews the very wrath of God in the form of pogroms, massacres, and Holocausts. The attempt of Eurochristians to dehumanize Jews then (and now) or the attempt of Eurochristians to dehumanize liberals now simply reinforces the fact that those engaged in dehumanizing the Other end by dehumanizing themselves.

Euroamericans are therefore in need of liberation. This is not an attempt to elide the suffering of those whom they terrorized and oppressed—either consciously or unconsciously. Instead, it is an attempt to recognize their self-imposed victimization when victimizing their Other. Those oppressed by Eurochristianity cry out for liberation. Those benefitting from the oppression, although they may not recognize it, are in desperate need of salvation.

Le Grand Remplacement

In the minds of Q devotees, as well as in the minds of some Euroamericans who repudiate Q, the apocalypse is already upon us. The end of the world began in 2020 as Euroamericans find themselves in a demographic downward spiral. Consider US Census demographic projections that estimate that by 2044, whites will cease representing the majority of the population, as nonwhites combined reach 50.3 percent.[13] Contributing to white anxiety are the population shifts made evident in the most recent 2020 census. Regardless of the attempts made by the Trump administration to hamstring the counting process, which led to an undercount of Latinxs, African Americans, and Native Americans while overcounting Euroamericans and Asian Americans, the end results nevertheless painted a portrait of a nation that is a lot less white.[14] For the first time, Euroamerican numbers dropped in absolute numbers, exceeding the estimates made by experts. Meanwhile, the Latinx population grew much beyond projections.

Nothing casts greater fear in the hearts of Euroamericans than the browning of the nation. The ember of this fear is continuously stoked by pundits, like Fox News personality Tucker Carlson who argues against *le grand remplacement*. Originally a historical anti-Semitic trope fearing Jews replacing Gentiles, this Great Replacement racist conspiracy theory was updated by the French white nationalist Renaud Camus (b. 1946) who argued that a global elite is seeking to replace the European white population with nonwhite people. Two hostile worldviews—anti-Semitism and racism—gave birth to the belief of "white genocide," otherwise known as the Great Replacement. Giving this anti-Semitic/racist ideology an American spin, Tucker argues that the Democratic Party wants to "replace the current electorate" with "more obedient voters from the third world."[15]

As the United States began to deal with its racist past by removing offensive Confederate monuments honoring those who fought for the bondage of Blacks—statues mostly erected at the start of Jim and Jane Crow to serve as intimidating symbols; as the Confederate flag was being officially lowered for the last time—recognized as a sign signifying terrorism; as Eurochristians argued Christ was being taken out of Christmas—being forced to instead say "Happy Holidays," Euroamericans fought back. Real Americans, true patriots, are being replaced, thanks to globalists (supposedly foreign and mostly Jewish) who are facilitating an immigration invasion and engaging in voter fraud.

This explains why the white nationalist who organized the Charlottesville rally praised Tucker's replacement comments,[16] piercing the night air chanting "Jews will not replace us." The Great Replacement became the justification for the El Paso massacre, according to the manifesto left behind on 4chan. This replacement theory has become mainstreamed as several congressional leaders began peddling Carlson's delusions. According to Congressman Matt Gaetz (R-FL)—who is under federal investigation for sex trafficking: "[Carlson] is CORRECT about Replacement Theory as

Great Replacement is embraced by both Left & Right

he explains what is happening to America." Congressmen Brian Babin (R-TX) adds, "They want to replace the American electorate with a Third World electorate that will be on welfare."[17] Senator Ron Johnson (R-WI) asked why the Biden administration wanted "complete open borders. . . . Is it really that they want to remake the demographics of America to ensure that they stay in power?"[18]

Euroamericans, fearful of being minoritized and disenfranchised, experience a deepening level of despair, helping explain the militant response on January 6th. According to a study conducted by Robert Pape, a political scientist from the University of Chicago, "the most interesting characteristic common to the insurrectionists' backgrounds has to do with changes in their local demographics: Counties with the most significant declines in the non-Hispanic White population are the most likely to produce insurrectionists who now face charges."[19] According to a study published in *Psychological Science*, Euroamericans holding differing political affiliations, when told of the 2010 Census Bureau conclusion of whites being a minority by 2044, interpreted the data as a perceived threat to their social status, leading to strongly supporting and endorsing political conservatism and the Republican Party while showing greater preference for their own race and expressing more negative racial attitudes.[20]

The belief, embraced by the Left, is that when whites cease to be a majority and the nation becomes more diverse, racism will cease to be a problem. While the future may be a nation that lacks a majority race or ethnicity, white supremacy, in the form of apartheid, will endure. Rephrasing and repurposing Mark Twain's supposed quote: "Reports of the death of white supremacy are greatly exaggerated." Any utopian post-racist future is pure fantasy, a false hope for the Left and a cause for fear for the Right. Because Euroamericans dread the supposed arrival of a 2044 diverse nation, the white minority issues a call to arms, a drumbeat by Republicans to facilitate a flocking to an already mostly white political party. Euroamericans live in mortal terror that when—not if—whites cease to be a majority, people whom they have oppressed for centuries will visit upon them all the same hatred and all the same violence. They believe people of color are as primitive, savage, and barbaric as Euroamericans have historically been in treating those relegated to their margins. They fear a karma where they would be the ones reduced to second-class citizens. This myth, this fear Euroamericans have of those on their margins rising in righteous revenge has been perpetuated since the foundation of the nation. We see this fear take root with the emergence of the "Lost Cause" interpretation of the Civil War as the Klan became fearful of those formerly enslaved becoming the new masters.

In reality, Euroamericans have little to fear. Whiteness will adapt to the pending browning of America because it is, and always has been, an elastic social construct. Prior to the colonialization ventures, people were separated by people groups. There was no white or Black, you were described by your nationality: the French, the English, the Germans, the Africans. Some five hundred years ago, to justify the profitability of colonialism and slavery, a person's worth and intelligence began to be determined by a lack of melanin. Some who were originally excluded from the definition of whiteness came to be included. At first, the "swarthy" Germans were not considered white. Benjamin Franklin, as we noted, warned of the danger their migration posed to Pennsylvania, for "[they would] never adopt our language or customs, any more than they can acquire our complexion."[21] For early America, only the Saxons and the English were white. The Irish, Jews, and Italians were also not seen as white. But as their children rose in political clout, becoming policemen and politicians, they did begin to be considered white, adopting mid-century anti-immigrant stances, and supporting segregation. They earned the right to be white when they learned how to say in English "n*gger."

No doubt before 2044, we will see those today seen as nonwhites also become white, like the Germans, Irish, and Italians before them. Think of light skinned Latinxs, specifically Cubans, who have expressed pro-Trump views and have participated in the colorism prevalent throughout Latin America. After all, Cuba had its own Ku Klux Klan Kubano

(KKKK), founded in 1928 in Camagüey.[22] While Latinxs face discrimination and oppression in this country, it should not be forgotten that those constructed as white in their nations of origins were as racist toward their darker compatriots as are Euroamericans. For example, the KKKK argued that the "negro . . . has been increasing like a malignant plague, demanding rights which he has carried to the extreme, SUCH AS THE POSSESSION OF WHITE WOMEN."[23] Attitudes of light-skin Latinxs can become more simpatico with Euroamericans than with other Latinxs who possess more indigenous or African features. For this reason, marginalized communities must spend as much time dismantling racist, sexist, and homophobic views from within their own community as they do in their struggle against the dominant oppressive structure under which all who are not Euroamericans live. The danger exists that some Latinxs will become Euroamericans, seduced by the illusion of assimilating to a supposedly superior and privileged culture.

The elasticity of whiteness becomes obvious when we look at recent Census reports: 1.2 million Americans who identified as Hispanic or Latino during the 2000 Census checked off "other race," only to change it to "white" during the 2010 Census, and for a large portion, back to "some other race" in 2020. Time will tell if Latinxs, whose identity usually wanes with each successive generation, will eventually become white again.[24] Some have made this transition more permanent. Think of Senators Marco Rubio and Ted Cruz, or of Proud Boys leader Henry "Enrique" Tarrio. It is telling that by 2020, according to a Wall Street Journal poll, the Latinx vote was evenly split at 37 percent between both political parties in the choice for Congress (22 percent undecided), no longer favoring Democrats.[25] If other light-skinned Latinxs continue to follow them, then whites, along with Latinxs who also identify as white, will—according to Census Bureau projections—represent 68 percent of the US population in 2060.[26] White would not become a minority in 2044, but a comfortable majority instead. Other groups might also be absorbed into the construct of whiteness if they are racially ambiguous Asians or Native Americans who embrace white supremacist political ideology. But acceptance into whiteness does not necessarily mean receiving the privileges that come with whiteness. Consider Jews who may check off the white Census box but continue to face anti-Semitism.

To make America great again is to return to that simpler time when such distinctions were not so complicated, and when whiteness simply dominated. The goal during changing demographics is permanent minority rule mainly through voter suppression, even if it means resignifying whiteness. Still, this will not be sufficient. As demographic shifts reduce the number of Euroamericans, intensifying with time, we can expect more Capitol-type insurrectionists if they do not politically get what they believe they have a birthright to. Feeling betrayed by their own government, and in danger of losing the white affirmative action that always secured their privileged space within society, Euro-christians, as we saw on our television screens in real-time refusing to recognize the certification of the president-elect, will continue to be the greatest threat to democracy. The threat was so real that for the first time in history the Chairman of the Joint Chiefs, General Mark Milley, who was appointed by Trump and whose responsibility was to advise the president, took extraordinary steps fearing a potential coup. Milley, believing "this is a Reichstag moment . . . the gospel of the Führer," informally mapped out with other top military officials ways to stop Trump from overturning the election. "They may try, but they're not going to fucking succeed," he told his deputies.[27]

Violence when whites feel they are losing a grip on power is not a new US phenomenon. From the xenophobic 1840s Know Nothing Party that targeted immigrants and Catholics, to the resurgence of the Klan shortly after the First World War, to today's Great Replacement Theory and the Capitol insurrection, fear of losing white status leads to responses where violence becomes an appropriate strategy to be employed by self-named patriots. Participating in domestic terrorism, as we have seen from Charlottesville to the Capitol, seeks to usher in a societal collapse that wipes out political structures understood as being detrimental to white privilege. Terrorism is here understood as the employment of unexpected violence—both physical and/or institutional—for the purpose of either bringing about change (as in the case of foreign actors) or maintaining the current political structures so that change does not occur (as in the case of domestic actors). We are literally [race]ing toward Armageddon due to the failure of Euroamericans, thus far, in reestablishing apartheid.

Demonizing CRT and BLM

An obstacle to the continuation of white supremacy is any critical analysis of how racism operates; hence, those committed to said supremacy must silence this form of intellectual inquiry. Take for example the November 30, 2020, communiqué of the six Euromales who serve as presidents of Southern Baptist Convention seminaries. They "declare[d] that affirmation of Critical Race Theory, Intersectionality, and any version of Critical Theory is incompatible with the Baptist Faith and Message."[28] Al Mohler, president of my alma mater, went on to state: "advocacy [of critical race theory] has no rightful place within a Southern Baptist Convention seminary."[29] These are not outliers on the fringes of Christianity; they are doctors of the church occupying central Eurochristian thought, shaping and leading the intellectual development of the next generation of Euroamerican ministers. In all honesty, they are correct—they are speaking truth. Eurochristianity and critical race theory are incompatible. The uncritical self-examination of Southern Baptists specifically, Eurochristians in general, and the Eurocentric doctrines that undergird their faith, makes their theology and philosophy incongruent with the liberative message of the gospel or the critical analysis needed to bring spiritual healing caused by centuries of white supremacist teachings. Not surprisingly, no communiqué has ever been issued thus far by the Southern Baptist seminary presidents, nor the Convention, condemning QAnon conspiracy theories as being incompatible with their beliefs. Maybe this is because a recent poll found that about a third of white evangelicals embrace the accuracy of QAnon's most outlandish claims.[30]

Arguing that Eurochristian churches that discuss critical race theory are against the will of God provides political cover. Take for example televangelist Pat Robertson, who during a *700 Club* broadcast told his audience that critical race theory is a "monstrous evil" whose aim is to give people of color "the whip handle" over white people. When criticized for his remarks, Robertson went on to clarify. "People of color," he explained, "have been oppressed by the white people, and the white people begin to be racist by the time they're two or three months old, and that therefore the people of color have to rise up and overtake their oppressors.

And then, having gotten the whip handle—if I can use the term—then to instruct their white neighbors how to behave. Now, that's critical race theory."[31] The fear of people of color emulating whites is also expressed by Tucker Carlson who sees critical race theory leading to white genocide. "[How] do we get out of this vortex," he asks, "this cycle before it's too late? How do we save this country before we become Rwanda?"[32] Basically, critical race theory incorrectly became shorthand for any analyses that intersects race with American history. Such an inquiry, according to these opponents of critical race theory, would only teach students to hate America and each other, and worse, teaches white students to feel shame and hate themselves.

No, Tucker, no, Pat, that is not what critical race theory is! Rather than seeking to understand the pain experienced by fellow Christians of color, supposed siblings in Christ, by issuing a clear and uncompromising clarion call for justice, they, along with fellow Eurochristians, choose to perpetuate a cult of whiteness by embracing a white God, a white Jesus, a white liturgy, a white biblical hermeneutic, and a white theology that reinforces centuries of white supremacy. Rather than espousing a critical race theory that can lead to the salvation of Eurochristians, a salvation that requires the crucifixion of their whiteness upon that old rugged cross by renouncing the sin of white privilege to become a new creature in Christ, they instead choose to embrace the cult of Eurochristianity that leads them down the wide and easy road to perdition.

Individuals, like Pat Robertson for example, passionately condemn racism while ensuring the institutionalization of that same racism, preventing people of color from discussing the reasons why they continue to face oppression, even after the passing of antidiscrimination laws. If critical race theory is an academic attempt to understand why racism and ethnic discrimination persists regardless of Euroamericans professing and insisting they don't have a racist bone in their body, one is left to wonder why they are up in arms, denying the academic freedom of exploring systemic racism and ethnic discrimination. Robertson, fearful of some imaginary slavery karma, provides us the answer that will save America from some future dystopia of white subordination under "the whip" of the descendants of those once enslaved. He projects upon bodies of color the barbaric savagery Euroamericans employed to create the greatest empire ever known to humanity. Robertson believes people of color are like Euroamericans, and if given a chance, a chance that might be possible through critical race theory, they would do to whites what whites, since the so-called Age of Discovery, have been doing to them. This is what scares Robertson and his followers.

If Robertson and Carlson are misinformed, what exactly then is critical race theory? It has nothing to do, despite disinformation, with diversity training or so-called cancel culture. Critical race theory is a 1970s once-obscure academic analytical methodology whose roots can be traced to Derrick Bell, a law professor, who sought to understand why people of color continue to legally face oppression, and Kimberlé Crenshaw who spearheaded early academic gatherings to explore the intersection of racism and the law. If racist policies, especially in voting or housing, became illegal with the Civil Rights Act of 1964, they pondered, why then did discrimination continue? To answer this question, racism cannot be understood as biological, but as a social construction that was historically designed to further the privilege, profit, and power of those defined as Euroamericans. The overt racist laws of the past created historical racist frameworks that continue to be legitimized today by so-called race-neutral laws, traditions, customs, and societal ethos ingrained in every aspect of US life—normalized and naturalized through social structures, political systems, and religious institutions. Laws that are race neutral in language can still reenforce racial inequalities by the discriminatory way they are applied. Racism, thus, has nothing to do with feelings of bias or prejudices. Instead, racism is structural, woven into the institutional fabric of society.

Rebranding critical race theory was an intentional strategy designed to scare Euroamericans by claiming the next generation of people of color will become their oppressors with the full support of Democrats who advocate such radical ideologies. Certain issues have always been used by conservatives to frighten and anger Euroamerican voters so they can support their candidates. Known as a *wedge issue*, they are employed to get out the vote. In the past, wedge issues have included the fear of Brown immigrants invading white America, fear of gay people redefining marriage, the fear of transgendered people using the "wrong" bathroom. This playbook maneuver has proven electorally effective. The newest wedge issue has become critical race theory. Republicans, with the support of right-wing terrorist militias, have been wielding this wedge issue at the local nonpartisan school board level in an effort to energize their base, laying the groundwork for 2022 midterm elections and subsequent elections for the foreseeable future.

Take for example the far-right nationalist militia the Proud Boys, who filmed themselves being the spear tip that pierced the Capitol on January 6. They have quietly been receding from the national scene, instead focusing on the local level—town council gatherings, school board meetings, and health department Q&A sessions. After the insurrection, the Proud Boys—in a clear policy shift—decentralized by disbanding their national leadership in favor of being exclusively operated by local chapters. Such a move mainstreamed their brand of violent politics on the local level.[33] Not surprisingly, since this shift in focus during 2021, some

165 local and national groups have instigated scenes of local unrest (some of them threatening) in at least 100 school districts, of which in about half of those districts, 207 school board members faced recall efforts due to a critical race theory that was not being taught in public schools.

How then did this once-obscure academic theory become such a powerful Republican wedge issue? The person most responsible for the anti-critical race theory hysteria is conservative documentary filmmaker Christopher Rufo, who falsely claimed the theory had a Marxist undergirding. Such claims are a red herring. The argument that critical race theory is Marxist because it is heavily influenced by the Frankfurt School's critical theory, which relied on neo-Marxist thought, is laughable because both trends of theoretical thought have nothing in common with each other, except that both use the words "critical" and "theory." In a Twitter post he cynically spelled out what he hoped to accomplish. Seeking to update the worn-out term "political correctness," he wrote—in a moment of refreshing honesty—that "the goal is to have the public read something crazy in the newspaper and immediately think 'critical race theory.' We have decodified the term and will recodify it to annex the entire range of cultural constructions that are unpopular with Americans."[34] In his own words, Rufo "turned [critical race theory] into a salient political issue with a clear villain,"[35] becoming shorthand for everything Euroamerica found objectionable with academia.

Rufo succeeded in scaring Euroamericans with this misinterpretation, a misinterpretation unrecognizable to scholars who employ this methodology. In a Reuters/Ipsos national poll conducted July 2021, 33 percent of Americans believed critical race theory taught "white people are inherently bad or evil," or that "discrimination against white people is the only way to achieve equality." It does not teach or advocate these positions. And yet it has become a powerful counter to the Black Lives Movement, limiting how racism is taught, and a tremendous motivator to turn out the vote as 22 percent insist critical race theory is taught in most high schools, even though it is not.[36]

Rufo, during an interview on *Tucker Carlson Tonight*, argued critical race theory is a "cult indoctrination" that had "pervaded every institution in the federal government"—it has not. He ended his interview making a call to action. Watching that summer evening in 2020 was President Trump who reached out to Rufo.[37] An exchange between the two occurred, directly leading to the White House issuing a September 22nd executive order prohibiting all federal contractors from providing employees training concerning race or gender that promotes "offensive and anti-American race and sex stereotyping and scapegoating."[38] In response to a summer of Black Lives Matter protests for rampant police violence against African Americans, Trump ended racial sensitivity training among federal agencies, calling critical race theory "divisive, anti-American propaganda."[39] Diversity training became, overnight, a racist manifestation of critical race theory. By March 2022, Rufo's efforts led to sixteen states passing anti-CRT bills, as twenty states awaited approval of pending legislation. In Texas, the lieutenant governor, Dan Patrick, has vowed to eliminate tenure for all new hires at public universities and colleges to stop the teaching of critical race theory.[40]

Lawmakers are not the only ones led astray by Rufo's disinformation campaign. If the six Baptist seminary presidents are correct in dismissing critical race theory because, as they argue, racism is a product of individual bigotry—a sin, then the cure becomes conversion, confessing their sin, repenting before the white Jesus, and accepting his unconditional forgiveness. Only salvation in Christ will eliminate racism, a position that finds its roots in Billy Graham. Graham criticized Martin Luther King Jr. for seeking to end racism through legislation, specifically the Civil Rights Act. King may have had a dream that "one day little black boys and girls will be holding hands with little white boys and girls," but Graham believed such a dream was utopian, not possible in this lifetime; "only when Christ comes again will the little white children of Alabama walk hand in hand with little black children."[41] But if racism is structural and institutional, as critical race theory argues, then individual conversions will fail in dealing with, let alone eliminating, racism. Individuals like the six white seminary presidents can passionately claim, "we stand together on historic Southern Baptist condemnations of racism in any form,"[42] while simultaneously fortifying the institutionalized racism within Eurochristianity that has historically privileged them and ensure the seminaries they lead would never question the unexamined power nestled in their white praying hands.

Authoritarian-leaning sentiments and regimes have always thrived when the masses are kept ignorant. Election data demonstrate Republicans do poorly among college-educated voters.[43] Ignorance, which easily scares voters, seeks the safety of a strong disciplinary hand. What better way to hype fear and maintain ignorance than to present Euroamericans with the threat of being replaced, the so-called racist ideology of critical race theory. Take for example the 2021 Virginia gubernatorial race. Glenn Youngkin rode the fear of critical race theory to the state mansion, promising, "there's no place for critical race theory in our school system, and that's why, on day one, I'm going to ban it." Cynically citing Martin Luther King Jr.'s comments about judging the content of one's character rather than the color of one's skin, Youngkin vowed to end something that did not and never did exist in Virginia's schools.[44] Critical race theory has become a dog whistle, a bogeyman whose main purpose is to create fear and anxiety over the Great Replacement to garner support for the Republican Party. Those who insist racism is structural, in a twisted form of logic, are gaslighted, accused of being complicit with racism. To employ critical race theory in one's analysis becomes, in the minds of white America, a racist and stupid act.

When the chairman of the Joint Chiefs of Staff, General Mark Milley, stated before a congressional hearing that when it comes to critical race theory, "those of us in uniform [need] to be open-minded and widely read," Tucker Carlson responded by declaring: "He's not just a pig, he's stupid." One would think that an educated military would win wars. But to be open-minded, to be informed, to be educated, as General Milley claims the military should be, is incongruent with conservative values. Knowledge about a theory—whether you agree with it or not—makes you stupid; ignorance of critical race theory is preferred because not knowing makes you smart. What better way to buttress the Black Lives Matter movement than by denying the academic exploration of institutionalized racism while simultaneously recasting those advocating critical race theory as the true racists?

Silencing CRT

US laws, customs, and traditions—in our modern era—are enough to create a panopticon society where those falling short of whiteness self-discipline. But what happens when communities of color have the audacity to demand the same rights and privileges historically reserved in this nation for Euroamericans? They are demonized and silenced. One often hears that we should speak (or write) truth to power. But power already knows the truth; they simply choose to ignore truth to maintain their unearned status in society by silencing any contradiction to their worldview. This unfair advantage can be maintained if ignorance abounds. History must be whitewashed. The truth of how an empire arose by what was stolen and who was enslaved is hidden so that an illusion can be promoted that America was made great solely due to Euroamerican ingenuity.

Critical race theory threatens the myth by raising the consciousness of those who are best kept ignorant so that white supremacy can flourish and thrive. Although a powerful political wedge issue, it can also threaten the very foundations of America's systemic racism. Yes, the utility of silencing critical race theory lies in winning elections, but more important to the health and well-being of Eurocentric nationalism is its ultimate demise. Critical race theory must be silenced, even if it means passing legislation that tramples on the rights guaranteed by the First Amendment. Hence, the purpose of this book—and the first two of this badass Christian series—is, and continues to be, the raising of consciousness by speaking truth to the powerless. And for this reason, in many schools throughout the nation, it will be legally banned.

White supremacy is maintained by Eurochristian intellectual concepts that are sustained by codifying social and political structures detrimental to disenfranchised communities by way of a supposedly objective educational system. But whenever a teaching methodology is employed that could lead to the empowerment of the disenfranchised—as in the case of critical race theory—a concerted effort is made to silence the perspective of those on the margins by means of legislation or violence. What better way to advance ignorance than to transform the classroom into a space of indoctrination, a space that reinforces white supremacy? The (class)room is appropriately named, for it is indeed a room of class—a room where students learn the class they belong to and the power, profit, and privilege (or lack thereof) associated with said class.[45] Far from being an objective, neutral educational system, students who attend (class)rooms can either be conditioned for domestication or be liberated from existing social structures. The former occurs by outlawing the teaching of critical race theory, the latter by raising consciousness through the hearing of minoritized voices. The current fight to ban critical race theory is an attempt to ensure that students entering the (class)room remain ignorant of and docile to institutional racism, especially if those students happen to be of color. The educational system, in the hands of Eurochristian nationalists and the gerrymandered politicians they support, serves to normalize and legitimize power structures that undergird white supremacy.

Gerrymandering politicians, who know the truth as to how power works, have made critical race theory an obsession. Throughout mostly Republican states, bills have been proposed and laws have been enacted that prohibit the introduction of diversity training by state contractors, advocate for the banning of literature by authors of color who tackle racism, and/or disallow the teaching of critical race theory in public schools. These unconstitutional legislative actions operate under the belief that this so-called Marxist ideology teaches one race or sex is inherently superior to another race or sex. Some states, like Texas, ban teachers from even discussing racism, white supremacy, or current events in the classroom.

The legal provision that downplays, sidelines, regulates, or outright prohibits voicing ideas or worldviews contrary to the dominant culture falls under the category known as *loi mémorielle*, or memory laws. Memory laws safeguard a particular interpretation of historical events over and against all other narratives. Even though one of the better-known memory laws, which exists in sixteen European countries and Israel, prohibits promulgating Holocaust denial, other memory laws are highly problematic, like Article 301 of the Turkish Penal Code that prohibits insulting the Turkish nation, its government, or its national hero. An example of such an insult would be validating the Armenian Genocide of 1915. China's Martyrs Protection Act prohibits disparaging the memory of national heroes, thus outlawing any critical analysis of Mao Zedong. Memory laws like those of Turkey or China mandate a particular view of history that legislatively prohibits the discussion of other interpretations based on conflicting facts. Seeking what occurred is silenced as those questioning, fearing repercussion, self-censor.

White privilege is the ability to enact memory laws that institutionalize denialism by prohibiting the recounting of any history that makes Euroamericans feel uncomfortable. Thirty-nine US Senators are on record stating that history education that focuses on systemic racism is a form of "activist indoctrination."[46] Memory laws are being passed to whiteout critical race theory to protect the feelings not of the most vulnerable, but of the most powerful. Outrage among Euroamericans has led to demands for its elimination from the curriculum or to its ridicule. One no longer needs to wear a white hood. The social, political, and religious institution does it for them. To question inherent institutionalized racism is prohibited, which only reinforces the supremacism that since the start of the colonial process secured the privileges, profits, and power of Europeans through the sweat of another's brow and the strength of another's arm. Without any twinges to their consciences, they lift their open hands in thanksgiving to their white God to receive showers of blessings bestowed to *his* chosen, *his* New Israel. But woe unto those who refuse to put on whiteness, insisting instead to understand their predicament through critical race theory, for the God whom whites worship is indeed a jealous God who prohibits conversation. This white God whom Eurochristians are seeking to protect from critical race theory is the God of global conquerors, the God of enslavers, the God of genocides, the God of capitalists, the God who rejects free thinking. This is a white God who enriches those who made God in their own image with unearned treasures stolen and through the labor of all those defined as inferior.

If critical race theory falls victim to memory laws, what then becomes the alternative? The alternative to critical race theory is confederate race theory. MSNBC host Joy Reid tweeted, "Currently, most K-12 students already learn a kind of Confederate Race Theory, whereby the daughters of the Confederacy long ago imposed a version of history wherein slavery was not so bad and had nothing to do with the Civil War, and lynching and violence never happened."[47] Picking up on Reid's Confederate Race Theory, I argue this worldview is a spiritualized ideology rooted in American exceptionalism, which argues that unlike all the other types of people in the world, Americans—specifically Euroamericans—are exceptional. Alexis de Tocqueville is credited with first making this observation during his 1831 ethnographical study of the emerging nation. For him, there is something inherently different about the white people in the United States when compared to other countries. "Thus the situation of the Americans is entirely exceptional, and there is reason to believe that no other democratic people will ever enjoy anything like it," he writes.[48]

This exceptionalism has come to mean in the current partisan political divide a moral superiority held by Euroamericans. The opening words of the preamble to the 2016 Republican Party platform proclaims: "We believe in American exceptionalism. We believe the United States of America is unlike any other nation on earth. We believe America is exceptional because of our historic role—first as refuge, then as defender, and now as exemplar of liberty for the world to see."[49] The document goes on to declare, "We are the party of peace through strength. We believe that American exceptionalism—the notion that our ideas and principles as a nation give us a unique place of moral leadership in the world—requires the United States to retake its natural position as leader of the free world."[50] This American exceptionalism, which provides moral authority for the United States to be the self-appointed world leader is the same spiritual argument employed to justify the white supremacy that undergirded concepts like Manifest Destiny or Gunboat Diplomacy. American exceptionalism is Confederate Race Theory that we can define as an ideology based on fear—fear of those who are physically not white; fear that the savagery imposed on others will be repaid in like-kind; fear that replicating how whites treated others would lead to their loss of status in society.

When the voices of communities of color are silenced, when critical race theory is exorcised from the conversation, Eurocentric education for students of color becomes a form of conversion or reparative therapy, an attempt to impose and enforce a denial of the history and reality of minoritized communities so that all can instead conform to what the dominant culture deems normative and legitimate. No one seeks to "cancel" Kant, Kierkegaard, or Krause as normative Eurocentric worldview. What is sought is the refusal to accept the Eurocentric worldview as the universal experience for all of humanity. They may very well be foundational for Eurochristian thought—and bless their hearts—but they remain foreign to the perspectives of those who have a different worldview. And while such scholars may very well make important contributions to Eurochristianity, their scholarship nonetheless remains damning to nonwhites because of how they are read. They fundamentally seek to cancel the thinking of those on their margins by colonizing the minds of communities falling short of whiteness, teaching those on the margins of Eurocentrism to see and define themselves through the gaze of the colonizers.

Euroamerican education as conversion therapy for the disenfranchised assigned to its (class)rooms is damning as the slew of conservative legislation is being considered and/or enacted to silence those who focus education on diversity. And let us be clear, political Euroamerican liberals are not the saviors, nor do they necessarily have the answers. In dualist thinking, Euroamerican liberalism is not the preferred alternative to Euroamerican conservatism. Liberal education is also damning to the oppressed. Not long ago, a student at a supposedly liberal Northeastern Ivy League divinity school boasted that those attending this institution were not being trained to be ministers, but bishops—so much for becoming humble servants of God. The room of class in this particular seminary becomes the gateway to ecclesiastical power. While the institutionalized racism in such liberal Ivy League institutions has been well documented, seldom do we consider that such schools are designed to teach those in their (class)room who are privileged to increase what they already have at the expense of those who lack the means of attending these same (class)rooms. And worse, so many academicians of color have come to believe that to be hired by such Ivy League institutions becomes the ultimate validation of their scholarship, failing to realize they will never hire truthtellers whose teachings subvert the very (class)room from which the Ivy school draws its power.

Because these students can afford exorbitant tuitions to attend particular rooms of class located on prestigious Ivy League campuses, they are privy to certain opportunities normally denied to those of lower economic classes, those more often than not students of color attending local community colleges (as did this author). Education has the potential of becoming the great equalizer. But education has been monetized. Regardless of how liberal Ivy League schools claim to be, they are far from the objective, neutral educational system they tout. A corrective to the educational system, conservative *and* liberal, is tapping into the wisdom of the marginalized, all too often ignored and dismissed as ignorant or arrogant. And when faces of darker complexion are sought out, all too often they are expected to wear white masks. To willingly, in solidarity, learn from the wretched of the earth requires effectively struggling against the (class)room training of Euroamerican conservatives and liberals. To learn from those at the margins requires listening to their stories, hearing how they experience racism and discrimination.

Euroamericans fail to deeply listen because they refuse to consider themselves to be complicit with white supremacy sentiments. How could they be racist if they voted for a Black man? When Senator Lindsey Graham (R-SC) argued that "our systems are not racist. America's not a racist country," he validated his assertion by arguing that the elections of Obama as president and Harris as vice-president is proof that America cannot be racist.[51] Based on this logic, we should not therefore be surprised that opponents of critical race theory bristle at accusations that their move to prohibit its teaching is motivated by unexamined racist biases.

Those who voted for Youngkin to serve as governor of Virginia in 2021 cannot be racist even though he campaigned on a "parents matter" platform that demonized critical race theory. Why? Because they also elected a Black woman, Winsome Sears, to the post of lieutenant-governor. Surely white supremacists would never vote for a Black person. Right? This may have been true of how white supremacy operated in the last century, but its manifestations this century have become more sophisticated.

Those who support white supremacy, in a demonstration that they are not racist, will cast their votes for people of color who do not demonstrate stereotypical caricatures, nor articulate typical concerns emanating from marginalized communities. That is, those few who support white political ideology by adopting supremacy talking points, specifically the denial of institutionalized racism and the misguidedness of Black Lives Matter. What does it mean that Winsome Sears served as the national chairwoman of Black Americans Making America First? An organization "dedicated to making America First by promoting the Trump policy initiatives."[52] She does not believe racism is systemic. In her mind, Democrat initiatives have coddled Blacks for way too long—to their detriment. The answer is simply to pull oneself up by one's bootstraps. This helps explain her opposition to critical race theory. Although she is a Jamaican immigrant, she nonetheless capitalizes on the fear of immigrants. Defending so-called biblical marriage, Sears embraced Eurochristianity.

Voting for Black Republicans who stand against the Civil Rights legacy and the current Black agenda derived and updated from said legacy does not provide absolution for Euroamerican racists. As long as these few who are Republicans do not make Euroamericans feel uncomfortable about their unexamined and unearned status, they can be supported in their quest to wear white masks. And as long as they embrace Trumpism with their white voices and colonized minds, they can even become a preferable alternative to white Republican candidates for that same office. Why? Because their election becomes proof that those who voted for a white supremacist political agenda cannot possibly be racist.

Going a step further, not only do Euroamericans believe they are not complicit with racism, they believe they are the true victims of racism. A greater lie than the 2020 stolen election is the proposition that those greatest oppressed today in the United States are white males. Regardless of which governmental statistical analysis one wishes to employ that demonstrates who receives less pay for the same work, who is most likely to be murdered by the police due to their skin pigmentation, who is more likely to live in ecologically hazardous areas, the argument that Euromales are the most oppressed is a lunacy that functions to create doubt. If white people are the real victims of racism, then the answer to their oppression is the silencing of critical race theory that is the cause. This leads to some very weird pronouncements, like Governor Ron DeSantis (R-FL) fashioning himself as the Martin Luther King Jr. of white people fighting against "cultural Marxism" and the "Black communism" of critical race theory.

At a December 2021 rally, DeSantis, who was introduced by a Euroamerican Black woman, proposed following nine other states in codifying a ban on critical race theory through his Stop WOKE Act. Seeking to outdo other states, he proposed legislation to allow parents to sue school districts if they teach critical race theory, and recoup any legal fees incurred. Additionally, diversity training by corporations would be banned because it "creates a hostile work environment" for whites. Unlike King Jr., who sought to unify the nation under equal rights for all, DeSantis's legislation stokes resentment against Black Lives Matter, which he calls a "radical organization." Terms like "equity," in DeSantis's mind, contribute to this hostility. "Just understand," the governor explained, "that when you hear 'equity' used, that is just an ability for people to smuggle in their ideology. . . . no taxpayer dollars should be used to teach our kids to hate our country or hate each other."[53]

Don't Look Up

Ignorance is unsustainable, for its continuous celebration will lead to the ruin of both the individual and the society. Society today is threatened with a crisis of reality, threatened when $2 + 2 = 5$—à la Orwell—becomes a viable truth. To insist on the reality that $2 + 2 = 4$ frightens the ignorant few while placing the lives of those who embrace truth and science in danger. Raising consciousness leads to harm, if not death, at the hands of the ignorant who are made afraid by manipulative politicians. Take the example of Dr. Allison Berry, a trained biostatistician and epidemiologist who served as the local health officer in Port Angeles, Washington. When the Delta variant spiked in her community, she implemented a mask mandate and ordered vaccination for indoor dining. The response was swift as protestors showed up at her home. Calls were made to attack her "on sight," warnings that "we are coming for you," as an appeal was made to reinstitute public hangings.[54] Dr. Berry's experience was not an isolated case. Think of the plot to kidnap Michigan Governor Gretchen Whitmer by six Euromales of a Michigan militia because of her efforts to contain the spread of Covid. We find ourselves, as a people, on the threshold of a violent cultural revolt against reality.

If the core message of Jesus is the giving of life, specifically, "I have come to give life and give life abundantly"

Questioning
Fauci =
white
supremacy

(John 10:10), then anything that leads to death signals an antichrist ideology. Which ideology, which worldview contributes to the flourishing of life, and which toward a culture of death? Everyone may have a right to be as ignorant as they want, but what we are witnessing today is the imposition of this ignorance upon public policy that only expands the insatiable hunger of the Grim Reaper. Ignorance, and the lies that it fosters, kills. And the political party that has become fertile ground for these lies and conspiracies to take root has become the party of death. Take the Covid pandemic as an example of the signs of the times.

The celebration of ignorance was best demonstrated when Dr. Anthony Fauci employed the most advanced and reliable science and most updated projections available to forecast a credible unfolding of the coronavirus pandemic. Despite his decades of experience as an immunologist, he was dismissed as a hoax, a "global fraud" by Fox television personality Tucker Carlson. The character assassination was designed to create the illusion in the minds of Euroamericans that Fauci's scientific conclusion was no more valid than the disinformation advanced about the virus, lies advanced by those who should know better. Even though a wealth of evidence exists that treating the virus with medicine used to combat malaria is both ineffective and dangerous, celebrity physician and eventual Senate candidate Dr. Oz became the remedy's chief promoter on Fox News.

Such disinformation, along with homemade remedies and the power of prayer, contributed to over seven hundred thousand US Covid deaths by October 2021, surpassing the 1918 influenza pandemic. This equates to one in five hundred Americans who have died from Covid!

The vaccines developed are almost 100 percent effective in preventing a severe case of the illness. This means that nearly every death that has occurred once the vaccine became available was preventable and needless. Health experts insist that the best protection against the virus is vaccination and mask wearing, but only 54 percent of the population was fully vaccinated when we hit the 700,000 milestone. Why? Because ignorant ideology trumps science. The science that has led to an effective antidote to the coronavirus is dismissed for ivermectin, an animal deworming drug popularized on social media, podcasts, and talk radio. Even though it led to death due to overdoses, the rush for the animal drug created a nationwide shortage.[55]

Ironically, our ancestors who lacked the scientific advances we have today showed greater intelligence and wisdom. During the 1347–52 CE bubonic plague that decimated the global population, certain truths were learned and practiced. Even though the time is referred to as the "Dark" Ages, our predecessors seem to have been more enlightened than some today. Concepts like quarantine and face covering were discovered to ward off the deadly disease. No one spoke about the loss of their rights or the imposition of some nanny state; they simply followed the proven science of their time not just for themselves but for their community to save lives. Our medieval ancestors must be shaking their heads in bewilderment over the ignorance that runs rampant today. We have an antidote at our disposal but abandon protection to remain faithful to ignorant ideology.

Some today believe that if a woman stands near someone vaccinated, she is at risk of having her menstrual cycle disrupted, or if she is pregnant, having a miscarriage. Others believe microchips engineered by Bill Gates are found in the vaccine, making people magnetic. Centner Academy, an education institution in Miami, Florida, warned children attending that if they hug their vaccinated parents for more than five seconds, they would be in jeopardy of harmful vaccine shedding.[56] Who needs a world-renowned physician-scientist and immunologist providing advice concerning a raging pandemic when a cacafuego suggests injecting disinfectants as a cure?[57] As a hard-core group ignores Dr. Fauci and refuses to take the vaccine, a large number of people, according to the American Association of Poison Control Centers, were accidentally poisoned with disinfectants from following the former president's advice, skyrocketing by 121 percent over the eight days following his comments and by 69 percent over the next ten days.[58] Science-based, educated experts are dismissed as a public chooses to celebrate ignorance, cozened by knaves looking out for their own self-interest.

Some Eurochristian ministers—like Florida Pentecostal pastor Rodney Howard-Browne, former Alabama Senate candidate and pastor Roy Moore (who lost his race over allegations of sexual misconduct with underage girls), and R. R. Reno, editor of *First Things*, the right-wing Catholic-aligned journal—have insisted that a hedge of protection from the virus surrounds true believers. Multiple preachers have insisted on holding in-person services, thus endangering their flock, claiming faith in God will defeat the virus. Because the virus, in their minds, is a hoax, only supernatural means will defeat it, and not healthcare policies.[59] Take pastor Scott Erickson of the Peoples Church in Salem, Oregon, as an example. After a Covid outbreak occurred at his church infecting seventy-two members, including him and his wife, he returned to the pulpit, preaching he would not kowtow to community pressure to close the doors to the house of worship.[60] These death-causing attitudes have made Eurochristianity the incubator of ignorance and death, taking many forms within the body politic. We would be in error to blame God for Eurochristian ignorance. When these Eurochristians claim their death-dealing actions as faithfulness to God, they are engaging in blasphemy. To say faithfulness to God requires allegiance to ignorance violates the first commandment by taking the name of the Lord in vain.

Ignorance is profitable. Sheep can best be fleeced with false teachings. Right-wing Eurochristian prosperity-gospel televangelist Kenneth Copeland begged his followers to make donations to his ministry so that he could maintain his private jet. He did not want to deal with the hassles of travel that require safety protocols like masking. For him, the "mark of the beast" is the Covid vaccine.[61] We would be mistaken to dismiss Copeland as an ignoramus. Frankly, he is as wise as a fox. His followers who are sending him money to maintain private jets are the ones who are idiots.

How then does one engage in an adult conversation with those living in a world of lies and conspiracy theories? When ignorance becomes part of the political discourse, one can expect devastating, if not damning results. Take for example Governors Abbott (R-TX) and DeSantis (R-FL) fighting school masking. They have chosen to offer up the schoolchildren of their states as living sacrifices upon the altar of presidential hope, making their prolife claims a cynical ploy. Not wearing a mask, not social distancing, and refusing the vaccine has become a litmus test for Republican fidelity and Eurochristian faith. According to a Pew study, of the 41 million white evangelicals in the United States, 45 percent of them said, as early as February 2021, that they would not be getting the vaccine, making them the least likely demographic group to be vaccinated.[62] The Republican Party has become the party of death for the very Euroamericans it strains to privilege.

Obviously, ignorance is a nonpartisan issue. But it appears Republicans have breathed in idiocy more so than Democrats when it comes to their response to the Covid pandemic. According to the US Centers for Disease Control and Prevention, unvaccinated persons are ten times more likely to test positive and twenty times more likely to die from a Covid infection when compared to fully vaccinated people who have gotten the booster.[63] And yet, the Republican Party has become more hostile to science, an attitude embraced by many of their congressional leaders. We speak of a vaccine hesitancy as the major cause of the August/September 2021 spike in cases and deaths, but the truth of the matter is that it wasn't so much vaccine hesitancy as it was partisan hesitancy. While at first, due to institutionalized racism and ethnic discrimination, African Americans and Latinxs lagged behind Euroamericans in obtaining the vaccine (and they still did by the Fall of 2021), the gap began to narrow as the partisan gap grew. During the third spike of cases, every reliable Blue state had a larger vaccination rate than every reliable Red state. Because liberals are getting vaccinated, conservatives, according to a Pew study, are more likely to get gravely ill or die from the virus.

In counties where Trump won by 70 percent of the vote, the death count from June through August 2021 was forty-seven out of every one hundred thousand. Compare this to counties where Trump only garnered 32 percent of the vote where the death count was ten out of one hundred thousand.[64] And of course, the real irony is that former president Trump, along with every Republican governor—including Abbott and DeSantis—got their vaccines. But risking one's life by not getting the vaccine is taking a perverted political stance. During a December 2021 interview with Bill O'Reilly, the former Fox commentator who lost his job over sexual misconduct allegations, Trump stated he was vaccinated and had his booster. He was met with boos from the audience.[65] Even as some lay in their deathbeds, their lungs full of fluid, making breathing a laborious task, they still insisted Covid was a ruse and pressured caregivers not to list Covid as the cause of death on their death certificates.[66] Ideology trumps what they were experiencing, a sure sign of cultish behavior. In short: stupidity kills.

5

Becoming Un-American

Throughout most of US history, this country has not functioned as a democracy. Instead, it has and continues to operate as a Eurochristian supremacist kakistocracy. Ignorance becomes an important prerequisite in maintaining this apartheid form of government that privileges one group of people—based on skin pigmentation—over and against all Others who fall short of whiteness. Consciousness raising in the form of critical race theory must be squashed so that alternative facts and conspiracy theories can provide tacit justification for the minority to rule over the majority.

This celebration of ignorance to muster the political power of the few is not solely a US phenomenon. In 1922, a few years after the Russian revolution, the Politburo gave orders to round up the intellectuals and place them in the infamous Moscow prison Butyrka and the Petrograd prison Shpalernaya. Most ended up being expelled from their homeland. When the Nazis marched into Kraków, their first task was not to round up the Jews, or the Marxists, or political opponents. The first laws they imposed were the gathering of intellectuals and placing them in internment camps. Because the greatest danger to any authoritarian government—either from the left or from the right—comes from academicians, they thus must be silenced. The most threatening and effective weapon against any authoritarian rule, over any claims of supremacy, is a decolonized mind whose consciousness has been raised to interpret reality apart from patriotic rhetoric or religious ideology. Consequently, academic methodologies like critical race theory must be outlawed in a so-called democratic society that advocates free speech. If being a patriot, a real American, includes undemocratic and authoritarian practices, then this chapter, along with the other two books of this series, unapologetically calls for becoming un-American.

Feast of the Epiphany

The January 6th storming of the Capitol was a Eurochristian nationalist and religious event. While Christians around the world gathered to celebrate the Feast of the Epiphany, some Eurochristians in the United States gathered in a half-baked putsch to overturn an election and advance a theocracy. While the Big Lie of a stolen election took root in the closing weeks of 2020, a protest in our nation's capital, called the Jericho March, began to take shape. The original march around Jericho, as retold in the book of Joshua, occurred when the Hebrews, after forty years wandering in the desert, entered the so-called Promised Land, land already occupied by the indigenous people. The invaders marched around the Canaanite city, blew their trumpets, and watched God bring the city walls tumbling down. The purpose of the DC march, in the organizers' own words, was to call upon "patriots, people of faith and all those who want to take back America" to travel to Washington to overturn the recent presidential election.[1] They came to the insurrection carrying "In God We Trust" banners, waving "JESUS 2020" placards, flying US flags embroidered with "Jesus is My Savior, Trump is My President," and brandishing the Christian fish symbol.[2] These rioters were not some American fringe element—they are America. True to their history of suppressing everything that is not white, they lifted both a large cross on the Capitol steps and gallows complete with a noose.[3]

Pressure was placed on Vice President Pence to overrule the will of the people by not certifying the election. Trump already warned Pence: "You can either go down in history as a patriot, or you can go down in history as a pussy."[4] But Pence, after exhausting all possibilities of staying in Trump's good graces, concluded his hands were constitutionally tied. This inconvenient fact did not deter the marchers that day.

Like Jericho, the hope, the goal was for the walls of democracy to come tumbling down. Some of the protestors even blew the Shofar—the ram's horn—not as a prelude to the three shevarim, but rather as a symbolic call for God to destroy the temple of the foreign god named democracy. One of the Shofars being blown that day was painted with the American flag.[5] For the God of Eurochristian nationalism is indeed a jealous God who refuses to have any other gods before it, like the god of free thinking, or the god of pluralism, or the most dangerous member of the trinity, the god of democracy.

Neo-Nazi Eurochristians, Klansmen Eurochristians, Proud Boys Eurochristians, Oath Keeper Eurochristians waving Confederate flags, brandishing the symbols of white nationalism, and wearing camouflage stormed the cathedral of democracy while singing the hymn "How Great Is Our God." Ironically, these hate groups who self-identify as "patriots" are the ones who the government deems to be the real threat to democracy. According to Homeland Security Secretary Alejandro Mayorkas, "[Domestic extremism] poses the most lethal and persistent terrorism-related threat to the homeland today . . . The January 6 attack on the U.S. Capitol and on American democracy is a searing example of this threat." The FBI agrees, going on to state that this "threat is persistent and evolving."[6] Rather than denouncing far-right Christian nationalists and white supremacists, the

Republican National Committee officially declared the riot as "legitimate political discourse." Trump even hinted that if reelected he would consider pardoning those prosecuted and convicted in the January 6 insurrection.[7]

Whenever white supremacist groups engage in horrific acts of violence, an attempt at gaslighting is made to excuse them by claiming their actions are no worse than acts imagined done by oppressed communities. For example, in the wake of the murder of George Floyd, mostly peaceful protests broke out throughout the country. And yet, right-wing groups like the Heritage Foundation painted a picture of roving Black thugs destroying American cities and being supported by then-candidate Biden and other Democrats.[8] Yes, there were cases when individuals acted violently, participated in the destruction of private property, and may have even participated in some looting. But these acts were the exception. According to a study analyzing all 10,600 Black Lives Matter demonstrations from May 24 through August 22, 2020, almost 95 percent involved peaceful protestors.[9]

But when Euroamericans stormed the Capitol to overthrow a legal election—chanting "Hang Mike Pence," threatening to shoot Nancy Pelosi, and forcing congresspersons to run for cover—congressional apologists began making a comparison between these white supremacist terrorists who sought to overturn an election and the Black Lives Matter movement that protested a state terrorism that marked them for assassination by law enforcement.[10] No comparison! Others stated the insurrectionists were but a conservative version of Antifa. It matters not that there is no such group called Antifa (it is more an *antifa*scist philosophy), unlike—say—the Oath Keepers who have an organization, membership, and leadership. Pretending an Antifa group exists, they were simply compared to Oath Keepers as two sides of the same violent coin. Antifa stands against groups like Oath Keepers whose goal is to overthrow the US government in favor of fascism. Started in 2009 by Yale graduate Stewart Rhodes as a response to the election of a Black man, the Oath Keepers refused to acknowledge the federal government's authority, focusing its recruiting on police and military personnel. They have taken up arms against the United States (i.e., Bundy's armed standoff in Bunkerville, Nevada, in 2014),[11] and more recently, several members face charges in their role during the January 6th insurrection.

Standing shoulder-to-shoulder with these violent extremist groups were dozens of Republican state legislators, congressional candidates, and local government and GOP officials.[12] White rage over a supposed stolen election was hyped in an attempt not to recognize the will of the people who disagree with them. This white rage led to unhinged violence in the form of 140 law enforcers (seventy-three Capitol Police and sixty-five DC Police) being injured that day as legislators hid in fear. Heads were smashed with baseball bats, flag poles, and pipes. One death of a police officer resulted from these attacks; two suicides followed.[13] One officer was dragged down the Capitol steps by several men who almost beat him to death. Among the perpetrators of this violence was Clayton Ray Mullins—a Eurochristian devoted to keeping his small Kentucky church financially afloat—who on that day was pulling on Officer Andrew Wayte's leg while he was on the steps being attacked. Mullins was engaged in a human tug-of-war with other officers trying to retrieve their colleague. With Mr. Mullins was Michael Lopatic who facilitated the capture of Officer Wayte when he grabbed another officer—Carter Moore—and began to furiously punch him in the head, allowing another rioter to grab Wayte by the torso and drag him down the steps.[14] Blue Lives do not Matter if they stand in the way of preserving white supremacy.

The rhetoric that America has always been a democracy seldom matched the practice. Unfortunately for those relegated to the margins of white supremacy, democracy was always understood to be reserved for Euroamericans. And here is the irony. These white supremacists smeared their feces[15] on the wall of the citadel of US democracy, built by enslaved Blacks as a temple to white men's liberty. Democracy is fine, and even desired, if it does not interfere with white supremacy. But if democracy, with time, spreads to those who originally were excluded from the American experiment, then it must be overturned in the name of God and country.

As horrific as the images of the storming of the Capitol were, the true terror is the cover-up that followed as the Republican Party did everything possible not to investigate what actually occurred and who was responsible. Some, like Representative Andrew S. Clyde (R-GA), argued that the insurrectionists were simply tourists.[16] Such responses have led Representative Liz Cheney (R-WY) to confess, "I do not recognize those in my party who have abandoned the Constitution to embrace Donald Trump. History will be their judge."[17] We are witnessing a breakdown in federal authority as two warring factions have become more entrenched in their Red and Blue enclaves. The political goal of white Republicans losing influence among the populace, coupled with shifting demographics, is to create a lock on power by doing everything possible, regardless of the cost, to quell dissent and distract from the violence that will be required to keep them in power.

Among those endangering democracy are former high-ranking political officials. Take for example General Michael Flynn, who was Trump's first national security advisor. Here is a so-called patriot who endorsed a Myanmar-type coup, suggesting the same should occur in the United States. When asked during an event attended by prominent QAnon conspirators if what happened in Myanmar could not happen here, Flynn responded, "No reason, I mean, it should happen here."[18] He suggested during an Oval Office meeting prior to the January 6th insurrection that Trump invoke martial law and deploy the military to "rerun" the election, an idea that intrigued Trump but was shot down by other aides in the room.[19] These insurrectionists, despite attempting to tear down the cornerstone of our democracy, see themselves as true patriots, real Americans. If so, we are left asking, What does it mean to be a patriot? What does it mean to be an American? To be an American means overwhelmingly supporting a man who expressed hostility toward nonwhites, disdain for women, hatred toward the undocumented, and cruel mockery of the disabled. White nationalist Eurochristians are the problem; Trump simply mirrored and reflected what it means to be real Americans.

Those who have lived on the underside of this America understand patriots as people who have always celebrated sadism. This is an America that took postcard photos of lynchings held during church picnics where everyone—men, women, children, and their religious leaders—unashamedly faced the camera and smiled. This is an America that exterminated Indians as if they were vermin, imposed slavery and Jim and Jane Crow on those seen as beasts, and invaded countries to the south occupied by those defined as uncivilized to steal their cheap labor and natural resources. Theft, enslavement, and genocide are as American as apple pie.

To be a God-fearing American, a patriot, is best demonstrated by storming the Capitol to protect and secure liberty for true Americans, to ensure their power, privilege, and profit are not now, or ever, threatened. Communities of color seeking equality in this experiment of democracy are, and always have been, a threat to Euroamericans. In the truest sense of the word, to continue supporting Trump and all his authoritarian leanings, to support the electoral college and other forms of voter suppression, is and has historically been to be an American. To embrace radical democracy where each person's vote counts equally and all people—regardless of race, ethnicity, sexual orientation, faith, or lack thereof—participate freely is to be un-American. The call of this chapter—and in fact this entire book—is to become, in the truest sense of the word, un-American.

This Is Not Who America Is

January 6th was not an aberration. Referring to then-President Trump, candidate Joe Biden would often claim: "It's not who we are, not what America is."[20] Biden, and many liberal Euroamericans, expressed shock at a president who openly expressed his misogynist and racist attitudes. They were dismayed at boldfaced attempts to employ the full force of the US government to remain in power after losing the 2020 presidential election. But what Euroamericans found difficult to accept is that Trump reflects the Euro-american psyche. Communities of color, on the other hand, living for centuries under the terror of racism and ethnic discrimination, had little difficulty in seeing Trump as an accurate representation of Euroamerica.

The contribution made by the Trump administration was to give Euroamericans permission to move away from political correctness and truly be themselves in public; to unapologetically be as racist, as anti-intellectual, as misogynist, as Islamophobic, as they wanted. What the Trump phenomena demonstrated, something that people of color have always known, is that the government—especially local law enforcement—cannot be trusted due to its inherent complicity with white supremacy. This is made abundantly clear by how the Proud Boys, comprised of street thugs, have been treated by police. When a protestor outside of the 2016 Republican convention practiced his constitutional right of burning the US flag, Joseph Biggs, who went on to be a leader within the Proud Boys, jumped a police line and started pounding the protestor. The police, it was later proven, falsified their report to charge the injured protestor with assaulting Mr. Biggs. A similar event occurred a few years later when Ethan Nordean, another future leader of the movement, knocked a protestor unconscious, only to have the injured party charged by the police with assault, even though the video of the incident showed otherwise.

This is a group that participates in political violence, which they film and post as a recruiting tool. A former official from Homeland Security, Elizabeth Neumann, captures the institutionalized racism undergirding how law enforcement approached this group: "If the Proud Boys was not a white male chauvinist club but a Black male chauvinist club, I think that, sadly, we would have seen a different policing posture."[21] Going a bit further than Neumann's thoughts, those who have existed on the underside of white supremacy know for a fact that if a group of men of color created an organization that engaged in violence towards political opponents, filmed said violence, and posted themselves terrorizing citizens, or if they were to breach the US Capitol and threaten Congressional personnel certifying an election whose results they did not like, they would be hunted down like dogs and put down. At the very least, federal agents would infiltrate the group, arrest members, and/or simply assassinate them. This was, after all, the strategy employed to disband the Black Panthers and the Young Lords back in the early 1970s. These organizations would limit violence, unlike today's right-wing militias, for the purpose of self-defense.

Law enforcement are not the only enablers of white hate groups. When President Trump was given the opportunity to repudiate the Proud Boys during the first presidential debates, he refused to denounce them, instead telling them to

"Stand back and stand by." To which the group responded, "Standing back and standing by!" And stand by they did, answering the call by the president to lead during the January 6th insurrection. They were the first to arrive at the Capitol (even as Trump was still speaking to his followers). They were the first to confront Capitol police and overturn barricades. They were the first to engage in hand-to-hand combat with police officers. And they were the first to breach the hallowed halls of Congress. Although the spirit of the Proud Boys has always been part of the American experience, true descendants of the perpetrators of violence toward non-Europeans who forged this nation, it would have been unthinkable in modern history for a candidate for the presidency from a major political party to voice opinions with which a hate group would find support and encouragement.

Regardless of Biden's protestations that "this is not who America is," Trump and his minions are the perfect reflection of the America that appears in the mirror, an America willing to vote against their best interest if it can assure the continuation of white supremacy. Even when policies are considered beneficial for all Americans, regardless of race or ethnicity, Euroamericans are in opposition if people of color benefit. They adopt a false zero-sum attitude that assumes anything that might be beneficial to communities of color must therefore be detrimental to Euroamerican communities. What made the era of Trump possible, an era that very well could reemerge in the near future with Trump or a Trump wannabe, and what could frustrate the Biden Administration ushering in a more just response to systemic racism and ethnic discrimination, is white supremacy.

The Greatest Generation Wasn't So Great

We have witnessed the apotheosizing of the so-called Greatest Generation, designated as great because of their endurance through a Great Depression and a World War fought against fascism on two fronts. The grandparents of Proud Boys have been referred to as the greatest generation; but maybe they weren't all that great. Maceo Snipes endured the Great Depression and bravely fought against fascism during the Second World War. He is not considered part of the Greatest Generation because he was Black. Shortly after returning from war to the town of Butler in western Georgia, he decided to cast his vote—for the first time in his life—in the upcoming 1946 Democratic primary for governor. The day after becoming the first African American to vote during the state's primary election, he was shot and killed by a fellow veteran, a member of the Greatest Generation, for the audacity of voting. These major supporters and enforcers of Confederate Race Theory are reimagined as the so-called Greatest Generation.

If the designation of greatness is solely determined by enduring and overcoming hardship and adversity, then yes, these Euroamericans deserve to be referred to as the greatest. But what if they also imposed upon others the economic distress and violence they endured? What does it matter to defeat the forces of anti-Semitism over there while continuing anti-Semitism and racism over here? What does it mean to replicate on the home front the fascist scapegoating that they defeated abroad? Can they really be the greatest while defending and profiting from the Jim and Jane Crow society many embraced when challenged by the Civil Rights Movement? Can a people be considered to be the greatest when bringing death to their Others? What do you do with a people who return from war to an America with the purpose and desire to maintain an apartheid political system based on the similar hatred possessed by the Nazis they defeated?

The Aryan master race ideology undergirding the Third Reich, defeated by the Greatest Generation, was maintained by laws influenced by the white supremacy ideology that undergirded Jim and Jane Crow. Anti-Semitic and the race-based Nürnberg Laws were based on, and directly influenced by, US laws.[22] But not just segregationist laws from the South. Nazi Germany also admired laws that dealt with the governing of American Indians, Puerto Ricans, and Filipinos. They studied Asian immigration restriction and regulation, and anti-miscegenation laws that existed on the books in some thirty US states at the time.[23] Nazi jurisprudence that led to the Holocaust was as American as apple pie.

After the war, returning GIs continued their own version of the Aryan master race ideology as the brightest among them joined the Council of Conservative Citizens (CCC) while the more ignorant found a home in the Ku Klux Klan (KKK). They and their children would stand behind Blacks sitting at lunch counters harassing them, plant bombs in churches as little girls sat in Sunday School, swing bats wrapped in barbwire on the Edmund Pettus Bridge, and perpetrate all forms of violence against those seeking civil rights. Their proud grandchildren would go on to support a president wishing to celebrate those returning GIs by making America great again, and when the nation chose a different path, stormed the Capitol to impose apartheid structures upon those not considered patriots. Should we therefore be surprised that most US citizens of color tremble every time they hear some white person pine for the America of the Greatest Generation?

The Greatest Generation must mean more than simply enduring and overcoming hardship and adversity. An element of bringing forth the cause of liberation for the least among us must be part of the equation that defines *greatest*. The label *greatest* must be reserved for those who endured and overcame the hardship and adversity imposed by the so-called Greatest Generation. Those who suppressed the voices and votes of the marginalized, those who denied economic opportunities, those who dressed in white sheets or pinstripe suits to impose fear to elicit compliance and do-mesticity can never qualify as greatest. The ones who should wear with pride the title of the greatest generation are not Eu-roamericans, but those whom they segregated, beat, abused, lynched, burned, disenfranchised, and subjugated through state terrorism. If we insist on defining greatest as fidelity and commitment to democracy and equality, then it is obvi-ous that the so-called Greatest Generation wasn't so great.

To make America great again is to return to a time when the Greatest Generation ruled. This is an America where Black lives do not matter, evident by the terror experienced every time an African American is pulled over by law en-forcement. Blue lives do not matter, evident by the number of police officers attacked and beaten on January 6th. Even white lives do not matter, as evident by the white protestors murdered in Kenosha, Wisconsin, by Kyle Rittenhouse (who was acquitted of the charges) because these protestors chose to be traitors to their race by standing in solidarity with com-munities of color. Simply stated, all lives do not matter, only a few. The only lives that matter, among the Greatest Gen-eration and their descendants, are those who support white supremacy and the reestablishment of apartheid.

I Like to Be in America

I—once an undocumented immigrant—am what former president Trump called "an animal," who "comes from a shithole country," bringing "many problems, crime, drugs, and rape."[24] This is how Trump and those Euroamericans who heeded his call to storm the Capitol see and define me. Even if I was to put on a Euroamerican mask to hide my Latino face, totally attempting to assimilate, real patriots would always "see" me with suspicion. True, they may place me on a pedestal to prove how they cannot be racist, highlighting Black and Brown faces that speak with white voices, but at the end of the day, I simply will never be fully accepted. I will always be—in their eyes—a spic. Therefore, I can never really become an American regardless of how hard I may try.[25]

But if truth be known, I do not want to be an American because it would entail embracing a history of enslavement, colonization, and genocide. The first step of any genocidal venture is to dehumanize those not defined as American. If the other is seen as an animal from a shithole country bringing problems, crime, drugs, and threatening the purity of white women—or better yet, are conditioned to see themselves through Eurocentric eyes, believing how they are being defined—then their oppression, their segregation, their extermination becomes easier to accomplish. Apartheid structures that have always kept us "animals" apart from the secure spaces of whiteness have historically been what it has meant to be an American.

To be an American patriot is to not care about the plight of the disenfranchised, employing all the tools at the government's disposal to segregate so-called animals from vanilla

171

Kicking out Liz's Cheney with supremacy?

suburbs. Racism, like a lung, or a brain, or a heart, is an essential organ of the American body politic. America as we know it today cannot function, cannot live without the poison of racism pumping through its veins. The storming of the Capitol on the 6th—not some past historical event a century or more ago—is the symptom of this ongoing dilemma signifying a diseased organ. A cure to what has ailed America can only occur through a complicated organ transplant, always a risky procedure that could result in the death of the patient. But to do nothing, to ignore what is rotting the American soul will nevertheless bring about death. Death of democracy is preferable for politicians representing the political interests of white supremacy, evident by the refusal to set up a bipartisan commission to investigate the Capitol storming or pass legislation that safeguards against voter suppression. They may claim Blue lives matter, but such pronouncements are disingenuous, empty rhetoric to serve as a right-wing counterpoint to Black Lives Matter. More important than investigating the cause of police injuries and deaths during the insurrection, protecting the white supremacist militias that stormed the Capitol takes priority.

And when some attempted to buck the white supremacist grip Trump has upon their party by refusing to drink the Big Lie Kool-Aid, they faced being canceled, best demonstrated with the ousting of the heir of the Cheney dynasty from House leadership,[26] or booing the 2012 presidential candidate and former party standard-bearer.[27] Seeking to call attention to the dominant culture's attempt to normalize and legitimize racism and ethnic discrimination throughout US social and political structures is demonized so as to distract from the attempt to institutionalize said racism and ethnic discrimination. To fight for justice and equality becomes un-American. And maybe it is because since its foundation, to be American never had anything to do with justice or equality. The sadistic elimination and extermination of those who fall short of whiteness has historically been the cornerstone of Euroamerican identity. To be un-American is to seek the liberation of those who have historically been relegated to the underside of the American story, a story that continues to be white, a story that continues to be undergirded by a Eurochristian faith that excuses the American way of injustice and inequality.

Toxic Hypermasculine Euroamericans

The greatest threat to democracy is—and has always been—Eurochristianity, a self-proclaiming universal hypermasculine movement. Should we therefore be surprised when a hierarchical masculine religious structure is congruent with a hierarchical masculine political structure? A male God rules in the heavens, a male (as ordained by God) cleric rules in the church, and a male rules in the family. Both the political and the religious operate under the shadow of the male penis. Hence the author of the letter to the Ephesians reminds those who lack the proper equipment of God's ideal hierarchy: "Wives, submit yourselves to your husbands as unto the Lord. For the husband is the head of the wife just as Christ is the head of the church, being the Savior of the body. Now as the church submits to Christ, so also should wives submit in everything to their husbands" (5:22-24).

Men have a divine right to rule, bestowed upon them by the ultimate male—God. Eurochristianity—since its foundation—has been modeled on a singular authoritarian figure, called to lead a people on the path of righteousness. Think of the divine right of kings that spiritually legitimized their political system. Kings ruled because God specifically chose them—and their hereditary line—to rule; therefore, to defy the king was the same as defying one's father, one's priest, one's God. Is it any wonder dictators and authoritarians love God so much because it is God's will that they rule? Are we really surprised that many ruthless right-wing dictators during the second half of the last century advocated family values, a positive term that masked controlling minds and bodies, specifically the minds and bodies of women?

Sadly, hypermasculinity was not exorcised from the church, regardless of women serving as clerics. The theology that brought us the divine right of kings has been updated to bring us a nationalist Eurochristianity that continues to embrace authoritarian rule. Hence, most Eurochristians reject democratic principles, and in fact many are willing to employ violence as the appropriate means by which to impose the will of God upon everyone else. According to a recent study conducted by the American Enterprise Institute, 79 percent of Republicans believe "that the political system is stacked against more traditionally minded people." And while the traditional American way of life is not defined by the survey, those on the margins recognize this way of life, based on history and experience, to be undergirded by a muscular racism and ethnic discrimination.

Still, we should beware of politicians who expound the traditional American way of life rooted in God, family values, or returning to the Eurochristian roots of the country. Such persons are dangerous because they use the symbols of the faith to galvanize nationalist goals. Hitler, Franco, and the Novo regime all embraced the cross to solidify God's calling upon them to rule. The Others—Jews committed to the Protocols of the Elders of Zion, militant Blacks, the Yellow Peril, Brown invading hordes, and godless communists, secularists, and atheists—contribute to the decay of the nation's morality, the downfall of the superior Western culture, and the supremacy of Eurochristianity as practiced by good normal and common people. In their minds, elites seek to reject God and elevate false ideologies like critical race theory. They must be stopped. Only the authoritarian can fix it, only the dictator can hold back the tide that threatens to inundate the true faith of the good patriotic Euroamericans. Should we be shocked that Trump, during the 2016 Republican convention, saw himself as an authoritarian wannabe, exclaiming, "I alone can fix it."

Rather than proposing ideas by which to deal with real political issues (recall there was no written 2020 Republican platform—except fidelity to Trump), cultural wars are invented to whip-up the Eurochristian masses. The man behind the curtain pulling the levers and turning the knobs rails against those supposedly seeking to cancel Dr. Seuss,[28] Mr. Potato Head,[29] and Snow White.[30] The party of voter suppression that failed to cancel the votes of people of color during the 2020 election has passed despotic legislation to cancel the votes of 2022 and beyond. These cultural warriors divert our attention from their attempt to establish an apartheid America by having us set our gaze on the supposed dangers of cancel culture and critical race theory. Such cultural controversies have drawn the line in the sand separating us from them, those fighting not to be replaced against those seeking to destroy the symbols of the America where Euroamericans lived before the onslaught of political correctness. The fight ceases to be against a political opponent with whom one disagrees, becoming instead a war to the death against God and those whom God has chosen.

To own the libs, Eurochristians must turn away from turning the other cheek, instead embracing a hypermasculinity by picking up the crusader's sword to silence and decimate infidels. The problem with America, in their minds, the obstacle preventing a God-ordained resurgence in the land is that men today are simps, too kind to women, suffering from low testosterone levels. "The crises of American men," according to Senator Josh Hawley (R-MO), "is the crises of the American Republic." Eurochristian nationalist Hawley—who seeks to take the "lordship of Christ . . . into the public realm"[31]—believes the Left want to create a world beyond men. "Manly virtues . . . the bright side of . . . aggression and competitiveness," are crucial for the health of the republic, and the Left's attack on "masculine values" has led to "more and more men . . . withdrawing into the enclave of idleness, and pornography, and video games."[32]

Hawley is not the only congressional advocate of toxic hypermasculinity. Consider representative Madison Cawthorn (R-NC), also a vocal Eurochristian nationalist. He has argued that "our culture today is trying to completely demasculate all of the young men in our culture." Why? "Because they don't want people who are going to stand up." Thus, he advises, "All you moms . . . if you are raising a young man, please raise them to be a monster."[33] Hawley and Cawthorn successfully harness Euromale anxieties of lost status due to a more diverse and equitable country. When we consider their role in the January 6th insurrection, their call-to-arms was for disgruntled young men craving perceived lost supremacy to take back their country and manhood by reestablishing aggressive and competitive masculine virtues. Hawley and Cawthorn are effectively offering them a sense of belonging and a purpose for existing.

The rise of the #MeToo movement was perceived as a frontal attack on toxic masculinity, a crucial social structure upon which all other forms of societal oppressions are based. The counter narrative becomes "Family Values" and "Make America Great Again," coded language for reinstating a Euromale dominance in the political system that can ignore rule-of-law accountability if it inhibits mastering those who are not manly enough. To become the man Hawley and Cawthorn call Euromales to be, domination and protection of those at lower stations in life is assumed, specifically women. It becomes the man's responsibility, his burden, to protect, educate, and lead those below his superior status. Implicit is the humiliation of women (grab them by their pussy) that becomes the paradigm employed to lord it over those seen as women by virile Euromales. The male virtues Hawley and Cawthorn advocate for are also about dominating the racial and ethnic Other—regardless of the Other's gender. The negation of those perceived as lacking testicles serves as a metaphor determining and defining, through the negation of the Other, who is a real man. In the minds of those striving to become the man Hawley and Cawthorn envision,

"I am what I am not. Men of color lack the qualities to be a real man. They are like children, like women. I am not a man of color; ergo, I am a man." The formation of the Euromale's ego creates an illusory self-representation through the negation of testicles, now projected upon Others, who are identified as non-Euromales. Ascribing femininity to the Other—regardless of gender—forces the construction of their identity to originate with the Euromale. In fact, those defined as feminine Object, in and of itself, are seen as nothing apart from a Euromale desire to possess, relegated to a castrated realm that reinforces their submissive unifying purpose.

As the nation's mores change, being a Euromale is not what it used to be. Who then should be blamed for their loss of power, privilege, and profit? Liberals are blamed, accused of seeking to feminize Euromales, while advocates of male virtues—like Hawley and Cawthorn—seek to do to liberals what Euromales have been doing to people of color for centuries. Not surprisingly, this call to manly virtues has led to the lawless masculinity demonstrated on January 6th, an attempt to reclaim a more muscular authoritarian political culture, rather than the more "sissy" form of government where all have equal voice. Euromales are granted permission to act upon their desires without fear of reprisal. Think of the collective yawn and lack of consequences demonstrated in the face of sexual harassment accusations against

Supreme Court Justice Brett Kavanaugh or Trump right-hand man and insurrection promoter Steve Bannon.

These symbols of toxic masculinity have become part of the American way—even embroidered on the national flag. We are left wondering what it means to sew the face of John Wayne on the flag. Or the face of Donald Trump. What new meaning is given to the concept of patriotism when the symbol of America, the flag, is merged with a symbol of toxic masculinity, whether it be John Wayne, Ronald Reagan, or Donald Trump? These three figures, a true Euroamerican hypermasculine trinity, embody and model an acceptable violence required in the pursuit of Eurochristian righteousness and law and order. And here's the irony. Those whom the patriots of white supremacy idolize—John Wayne, Ronald Reagan, and Donald Trump—all avoided defending their country when called upon by the military, even while creating the tough war-hero image. While Hollywood actors like Clark Gable, who was six years older than Wayne, or Jimmy Stewart, who was one year younger and ineligible due to his low weight, rushed to enlist and serve their country during World War II, Wayne refused, instead filing for a 3-A draft family deferment. Reagan's poor eyesight qualified him for limited service, excluding him from going overseas. The closest both came to seeing action was playing soldiers on a movie set. Donald Trump dodged the draft by receiving four deferments due to education and a 1-Y medical deferment for bone spurs in his heels—which many consider a made-up injury. He wondered why someone would serve in Vietnam and questioned their intelligence for not being able to game the system.[34] He would go on to say during a 1998 interview on the Howard Stern show that avoiding getting a sexually transmitted disease during the sixties was his own Vietnam.[35] All three lacked the courage to serve their country when called upon, and yet all three are idolized for their hypermasculinity, signifier of Eurochristian nationalism.

As more Euromales and evangelicals identified as Republicans,[36] violent political rhetoric escalated.[37] They advocate religious freedoms, but not for everyone. Religious freedoms become the exclusive right of privileged Eurochristians, becoming the freedom to impose conservative beliefs upon everyone regardless of their faith perspective, or lack thereof. In the name of religious freedom, reproduction rights and same-gender loving relationships are curtailed—with an eye towards their ultimate legal prohibition. Cowardly Eurochristians subjugate faith to the prevailing cruel political structures that seek to make Trump God's anointed. This Eurocentric manifestation of Christianity misconstrues courage and fidelity of faith with repression and oppression of those whom they deem nonbelievers.

And here is the ultimate gaslighting move. Even though Euromales are responsible for most of the mass shootings that have occurred in this nation,[38] it is men of color America has been taught to fear. To be a man of color is to be a threat to white America, especially white women. The angry Black man and the invading Brown man have become overly sexualized caricatures to be feared. Whether they be the thug or the bad hombre, the brute or the gangbanger, whites have been taught to be afraid of Black and Brown men. Think of how the defense attorney Laura Hogue, during the Ahmaud Arbery murder trial, sought to describe the victim as the stereotypical Black Brute to be feared, with "his long, dirty toenails."[39] Fear has been significant in justifying a terror campaign against all people of color at the hands of not just law enforcement, but average citizens who are at liberty to kill non-Euroamericans if they just say they feared for their life and were standing their ground. Stand Your Ground legislation exists to shield and protect Euroamericans when they kill people of color. When a group of peaceful Black marchers walked by the home of Mark and Patricia McCloskey in St. Louis, Missouri, they were met with firearms pointed at them by the couple under the excuse that these good white folk felt threatened by Blacks. Rather than being repudiated for their racist behavior, they were rewarded with a speaking spot during the 2020 Republican Convention and a 2022 run for the US Senate.

Since the Black Lives Matter protests erupted over the killing of George Floyd, Euroamerican legislators have rushed to make it easier to kill protestors, specifically protestors of color. Such laws, we are told, are necessary because groups like Black Lives Matter are supposedly violent. They burn, they loot—we are told. However, as previously mentioned, the vast majority of protests over the summer of 2020 were nonviolent. Based on incident reports, 96.3 percent involved no property damage while 97.7 percent showed that no police injury occurred. When there were violent acts—as reported—they were mainly documented as being instigated by either counter-protestors (think of the Boogaloo Boys) or police officers directed at the protestors.[40]

This obsession of legalizing the right of Euroamericans to kill those who challenge their privilege has taken a frightening turn when Republican legislators in both Iowa and Oklahoma passed laws that provide immunity for drivers who run over and injure protestors on public streets. Donald Trump is not the only one who can boast of shooting someone on Fifth Avenue and getting away with it. Anyone can shoot or run over a person of color, and by simply declaring they felt their safety was threatened, can probably escape prosecution. Other states are considering laws that will bar anyone convicted of "unlawful assembly" from holding state employment or elected office, while other states will deny them receiving student loans, unemployment benefits, or housing assistance.[41] Such laws are directed solely toward Black Lives Matter protestors.

Just imagine what would have happened if a person of color decided to ram their car into white insurgents heading toward the Capitol on January 6th, claiming the driver feared for their life. But claiming fear is only reserved for Euroamericans. Only they are provided a license to brutalize not just people of color, but other Euroamericans who stand in solidarity with the disenfranchised. Just remember how angry white men started the KKK as a response to Reconstruction or how they instituted Jim and Jane Crow to protect themselves and their women from the supposed menace of Blacks. Not much has changed as today's angry white men stormed the Capitol to institute a more authoritarian system that protects them from the menace of people of color voting.

Enraged Euromen are welcome news for right-wing politics. Ironically, some Republicans fear that there are not enough angry Euromen. Listen carefully to the words of Senator Lindsey Graham (R-SC) after the reelection of a Black man to the White House as to why Republicans are falling short of electoral domination: "The demographics race we're losing badly. We're not generating enough angry white guys to stay in business for the long term."[42] Night marches like the Unite the Right rally, or roving packs of angry Euromen like the Proud Boys—reminiscent of brownshirts a century ago—serve as foot soldiers in bringing about the masculine authoritarian political system for which they salivate; but true success in reestablishing an Apartheid America rests with state legislators.

Constitutional Crises

An Apartheid America is achievable when a minority of the population internalizes fascist principles. Philosopher Michel Foucault explained that "the strategic adversary is fascism. . . . And not only historical fascism, the fascism of Hitler and Mussolini—that was able to mobilize and use the desire of the masses so effectively—but also the fascism in us all, in our heads and in our everyday behavior, the fascism that causes us to love power, to desire the very thing that dominates and exploits us."[43] The internalized fascism Foucault describes resonates with the sanctity of normalcy that drives habituated obedience, a normalcy that made the storming of the Capitol legit.

If democracy is brought down in America, it will not be at the hands of foreign troops. The demise will be at the hands—as we saw on January 6th—of those with fascism in their hearts, waving the flag and praising the name of Jesus. Eurochristianity, masked as patriotism, will be the unapologetic culprit of bringing the democratic experiment to an end. In the minds of insurrectionists, it is God's will for the faithful minority, as God's true remnant, to disenfranchise by whatever means possible those they define as the godless heathen majority. The subjugation of unfaithful liberals, who are supposedly responsible for leading America into darkness (spiritually and socially), requires a Faustian compact

185

with Trumpism. For the first time in the history of the United States, a sitting president—with the support of the Religious Right—sought to overturn the results of a free and legal election. So-called patriots rejected the principles of maintaining and sustaining a democratically elected form of government because the only way Eurochristians can retain political power is by subverting the tenets of the US Constitution.

We find ourselves amid multiple constitutional crises, facing a coordinated attack by one of the two political parties on the legitimacy of our government. At the head of this coordinated attack to undermine the Constitution is the former president of the United States who, as of this writing, holds a vise grip on the GOP, a party complicit in a cover-up that refuses to exercise its constitutional authority to place a check on the executive branch of the government. Incontrovertible evidence exists that the former president and extreme Trumpish forces sought dominance in the political system, even if it meant subverting the very laws designed to serve as guardrails of our democracy. And while these Trumpish forces may have failed to overturn the 2020 election, they are laying the groundwork to subvert future elections.

The 2008 election of a Black man to occupy a house that was destined to always stay white was a wake-up call to the beneficiaries of white supremacy. For one of the few times in electoral American history, the voices of most of the people who have usually been kept silent expressed a vision of a possible future through the ballot box. This quickly became a crisis for Euroamerica. They could no longer trust the racially rigged election structures since the days of Jim and Jane Crow to protect and expand their place within society. Originally it was legally easier to maintain an apartheid system. First, only Euromale property owners could vote, then only Euromales. When Black males were also given the vote, the expansion of democratic rights were quickly curtailed. With time, laws were passed to disenfranchise their votes to the point that predominately Black districts elected white racist representatives. Voting rights were later expanded to women, but thanks to Jim and Jane Crow, only Eurowomen were welcomed to the voting booth. Black women faced the same obstacles as Black men.

Making voting difficult for people of color has always been an apartheid strategy employed since the foundation of the Republic. The Civil Rights Movement offered the hope that democracy might become a reality in America as the vestiges of segregation began to crumble. Soon, it seemed as if the tactics of Jim and Jane Crow would be relegated to history books. But the apartheid system that rigged elections to privilege whiteness did not disappear; instead, it became more sophisticated. No longer did the marginalized have to guess how many jellybeans were in a jar. Old apartheid strategies like the electoral college and gerrymandering were strengthened and expanded while new forms of voter suppression were enacted. Euroamericans would have confidence in the integrity of the voting process once the votes by people of color were suppressed. Obviously, the battle cry cannot be: "Deny people of color the right to vote." This may have worked sixty years ago, but it would be a hard sell today.

The new battle cry, which continues the tradition of suppressing the votes of people of color but sounds so much more politically correct, becomes: "Protect the integrity of elections." Suppressing the vote of the minority steals their voices, their rights, their liberties, and their dignity. Suppression becomes the alternative when a political view, in this case Eurochristian nationalism, fails to attract the majority of the population. Examine the leaked video of Jessica Anderson, the executive director of Heritage Action for America (affiliated with the Heritage Foundation), bragging how easy it was to "quickly and . . . quietly" craft voting restriction legislation throughout the country since the Big Lie—and "honestly, nobody noticed." She boasted of drafting the legislation for state lawmakers, or in some cases having "a sentinel on our behalf give them the model legislation, so it has that grassroots, from-the-bottom-up type of vibe," which masks the massive campaign to enact voter suppression in key states.[44]

Political power can only be obtained and maintained by preventing opponents—mainly voters of color and their allies—from voting. The Republican Party, as the party of Euromales and evangelicals, is on the losing side of demographics and history. As the population becomes more diverse, their ability to attract voters diminishes. Starting in 2013, election laws became, in earnest, weaponized, with the *Shelby County v. Holder* decision that dealt a major blow to the Voting Rights Act of 1965. Opponents of civil rights argued that Section 5 of the 1965 Act had outlived its purpose because racism no longer existed, especially since a Black man was at the time occupying the White House. Chief Justice Roberts referred to the protection as the "perpetuation of a racial entitlement."[45] The Supreme Court struck down the heart of the Voting Rights Act, freeing nine states to change their election laws without federal preclearance.[46] State Legislatures wasted no time in following the Supreme Court's lead, closing an estimated 1,700 polling stations throughout the South in areas that have had a history of disenfranchising voters. They redrew districts along the lines of racial gerrymandering and imposed discriminatory voter IDs. At the time, in a dissenting opinion, Justice Ginsburg wrote that gutting the Voting Rights Act was tantamount to "throwing away your umbrella in a rainstorm because you are not getting wet."[47]

Republicans lack the votes to maintain power. Rather than doing what most political parties do after losing an election, rethink one's platform and rebrand messaging to appeal to a larger, more inclusive audience, they have chosen to instead restrict and suppress voting of those who are not older Euroamericans. Republicans' only hope of success is to create structural advantages to win elections without the need of convincing most voters to support them. Even though Republicans have recently used the unprovable charge of voter fraud to pass voter suppression laws, the Stop the Steal campaign accelerated such legislation by creating distrust in the electoral system. Throughout 2021, those embracing the Big Lie introduced 440 bills in forty-nine states specifically designed to suppress the votes of people of color. Of those, thirty-four laws were enacted in nineteen states. These numbers are expected to increase in subsequent legislative years.[48] If the people question the integrity of the system, demagogues can arise to "fix" what is not broken.

Win at any cost becomes the mantra of Trumpish forces, even if it means burning democratic structures to the ground. Voter suppression strategies since the manufactured Big Lie are not some new phenomena, but an expansion of an apartheid strategy that has always been part of the US fabric. The success of suppressing votes, through passing apartheid strategies, was recognized by the Electoral Integrity Project, an independent international research group that studies and monitors the quality of hundreds of worldwide elections. In 2016, the year Trump was elected, the Electoral Integrity Project ranked the United States fifty-second out of 153 countries, behind all developed western democracies, making the US election system among the least democratic in the West.[49]

Both Democrats and Republicans are responsible for the nation's drift toward undemocratic principles. And while there are bad actors playing dirty tricks on both sides of the aisle, Republicans have become more brazen. Consider the words of Justin Clark who was the senior political adviser and senior counsel to Trump's reelection campaign, spoken privately to influential Wisconsin political leaders. Unbeknownst to him, his conversation was recorded. On tape you can hear him discuss how Republicans "traditionally" rely on voter suppression to be competitive in battleground states like Wisconsin. "Traditionally it's always been Republicans suppressing votes in places," Clark confessed. "Let's start protecting our voters. . . . Let's start playing offense a little bit. That's what you're going to see in 2020 . . . a much more aggressive program, a much better-funded program." Clark went on to express Trump's approval of these suppression tactics. "We've all seen the tweets about voter fraud, blah, blah, blah. Every time we're in with him, he asks what are we doing about voter fraud? . . . The point is he's committed to this; he believes in it and he will do whatever it takes to make sure it's successful. . . . Cheating happens at the margins. What we're going to be able to do . . . is focus on these places."[50]

In short, the entire debate about protecting the integrity of the vote is code language for protecting the integrity of the white vote. The rally cry to "count all legal votes, not illegal votes," is also code language for count all white votes, not "colored" votes. What 2020 demonstrated is the need to reinstate a Jim and Jane Crow 2.0, a kinder, gentler version of an apartheid nation. So, what are these "aggressive programs" to which Clark is referring? Different undemocratic legal strategies have historically existed to maintain an apartheid political structure, strategies that we are witnessing being strengthened to maintain minority Republican rule. They include the continuation of the Electoral College, the expansion of gerrymandering, tightening voter identification requirements, purging voter rolls, recruiting partisan poll watchers, restricting early voting, and changing the rules on how an election is called. In essence, finding a legislative solution for a problem that empirical evidence shows does not exist, laws have been passed to reinstate Eurochristian supremacy in the name of patriotism.

The Electoral College made it possible for a man with no political experience whatsoever to become president even though he lost the popular vote by almost three million votes, the third time this occurred in US history, the second time in this century alone. Thanks to a relic from slaveocracy, he was awarded the presidency. Six weeks after the presidential election, 538 electors gather to cast their votes. The ascent to the presidency by those who lost (Bush in 2000, Trump in 2016) is due to an apartheid-type political mechanism created during this nation's slavocracy. Not trusting direct democracy, the founding fathers (mothers were excluded from deliberation) cobbled together a last-minute convoluted compromise during the 1787 Constitutional Convention where people did not vote for the president, but instead voted for party delegates (even if only the candidate's name is on the ballot) who in turn would vote for the candidate that carried the state. This structure today disenfranchises millions of voters in about forty safe blue or red states where the outcome is never in doubt, making their vote worthless. The vote of a Democrat in Wyoming or a Republican in the District of Columbia for the next president makes no difference whatsoever to the outcome. Choosing the president is reduced to about 20 percent of the population who live in the five to ten battleground states. In a winner-takes-all structure, the candidate who wins the state's popular vote (except for Maine and Nebraska) is given all the state's electoral votes.

The result of the Electoral College for our current times is that after 1988, out of the past eight presidential elections, Republicans won the popular vote once (Bush's second term in 2004). Nonetheless, Republicans served as president in

Russiagate?
anyone?

three of those elections. Someone who loses the election for the highest office in the land can still be sworn in and change the course of the nation because we do not operate as a democracy, but instead as an apartheid system that privileges the minority view. When citizen Trump thought the 2012 candidate Mitt Romney, whom he supported, might win the popular vote but lose the electoral vote to Obama, he tweeted, "The electoral college is a disaster for a democracy."[51] Trump was right!

Al Gore won the 2000 presidency by over half-a-million votes; still, the Supreme Court ruled in favor of Bush in the close 50-50 popular vote split of Florida, thus delivering all 27 electoral votes, and the presidency, to Bush. Maintaining he really won the popular vote if not for voter fraud, Bush had the US Justice Department conduct a three-year study. The argument that whenever a Republican loses the presidential election it is due to fraud has been a consistent conspiracy theory voiced throughout the twenty-first century. They argued Bush appeared to have lost the popular vote because of voter fraud in the state of New Mexico, which went for Gore by a few hundred votes. Adding to the conspiracy was Senator John Ashcroft's (R-MO) reelection loss to a dead man (his opponent Mel Carnahan died three weeks earlier), which was supposedly due to Democrats cheating in St. Louis. The report commissioned by Bush concluded that out of all the votes cast during the 2000, 2002, and 2004 federal elections, only twenty-six individuals fraudulently registered to vote, or voted, representing 0.00000132 percent of all votes cast.[52]

This racist, anti-democratic quirk of the Electoral College also delivered the presidency to Trump sixteen years later. The reason the Electoral College is racist and anti-democratic is because it is skewed to give the votes cast by Euroamericans greater weight than the votes cast by people of color. For example, during the 2016 election, one electoral vote representing 508,000 voters from a racially and ethnically diverse city like Los Angeles was equal to one electoral vote from Wyoming representing 143,000 mainly Euroamerican conservative voters. The myth of every vote counting masks an apartheid that makes one white conservative Wyoming vote equal to three and a half racially and ethnically diverse liberal Los Angeles votes.

Trump won the Electoral College in 2016, even though Clinton won the popular vote by almost 2.9 million votes.[53] With 306 electoral votes, Trump won over Clinton, who garnered just 232 electoral votes. But winning the presidency was not enough. His ego could not handle the embarassment of losing the popular vote, leading him to launch a face-saving strategy of introducing a lie. Shortly after the election, Trump tweeted that he actually won the popular vote. The numbers, however, were skewed because "over three million illegals [*sic*] voted in California."[54] No evidence was given nor needed to be given. The burden of proof is not the responsibility of the one making the false statement, but those reproached.

Like Bush before him, Trump launched an investigation into supposed 2016 voter fraud.[55] Based on scholarly evidence, investigative reports demonstrated voter fraud was a minuscule problem. About sixty-three credible alleged cases of suspected fraud or 0.00000046 percent of all the votes casts were discovered.[56] These numbers appear to be the norm when compared to Bush's study earlier in the century. After almost a year of investigation, with nothing to show, the Presidential Advisory Commission on Election Integrity was quietly disbanded, and the accusation forgotten.[57] The influence of a president who failed to receive the majority of the vote of the body politic will last longer than the four years they served in office. Consider the influence the loser of the 2016 election had in reshaping the Supreme Court, an impact upon the nation that could last three to four decades.

Gerrymandering is a strategy employed when redrawing voting maps every ten years following the census count in a manner that privileges one political party over and against another. No tool is more effective in minimizing the representation of increasingly minoritized communities than gerrymandering. Imagine a state comprising just one hundred voters and five congressional districts. Of the hundred voters, sixty are Euroamericans and forty are people of color. Equal congressional representation would mean two of the congressional districts would lean toward representation from communities of color while three would be representative of the views of Euroamericans. But let's say Republicans, who tend to be white and conservative, control the state legislature and are thus charged with redrawing the political map. Fearing that people of color tend to be more liberal and vote Democrat, they redraw the map to minimize their voice. These Republicans can redraw the political lines so that each of the five districts have eight people of color to twelve Euroamericans, thus all five congressional seats are safely within the Republican column. This process is known as "cracking." But let's say Democrats control the state legislature. They in turn can redraw the maps so that two districts solely comprise Republicans, and thus reduce their influence to just two congressional representatives while increasing their minority party to represent three districts. This process is known as "packing."

Gerrymandering is a strategy employed by both parties, even though it mainly has negatively impacted communities of color.[58] Regardless of which side employs this strategy, it is antidemocratic because it allows legislators to choose their voters and create safe seats for themselves. The last redistricting conducted at the time of this writing, based on the 2010 census, demonstrates the implementation of an apartheid system that favors the minority of the population. A whitelash against the election of a Black man to the White House two years earlier led to Republicans flipping 680 state legislative seats and twenty chambers, possible with the financial backing of conservative businessmen like the Koch brothers. This electoral success was due to Republicans redrawing fifty-five percent of congressional districts to their favor and thus controlling national politics for a decade—regardless of a Democrat capturing the White House. So even though the 2012 election showed Democrats garnered a larger percentage of votes than Republicans, gerrymandering delivered the 113th Congress to Republicans.

The recent success of gerrymandering that gave the minority political party a majority advantage is due to a little-known redistricting expert, Thomas B. Hofeller, who played a crucial role in drawing the partisan maps of 2011. After his death in 2018, his work documented on his computer and made public by family members demonstrated how an apartheid political system for our modern times was constructed. For example, his emails show how he packed Democratic-leaning Travis County by moving 30,000 people with Spanish surnames—determined by SSVR (Spanish Surname Voter Registration)—from a Republican district. A trove of files demonstrate how he was the architect of Republican dominance in swing states like North Carolina by using racial statistics to make race and/or Latinx ethnicity a constant when drawing district lines on a map.[59] Due to a 2019 Supreme Court five-to-four decision,[60] federal courts are powerless to hear challenges to partisan gerrymandering even though racial gerrymandering remains illegal, ignoring how partisan gerrymandering is often based on racial and ethnic demographics. Legal partisan gerrymandering becomes the cover for illegal racial gerrymandering as future map drawers simply argue their intentions were partisan, not racial.

The 2020 state election results ensure things will get worse for the rest of the decade. At the start of redistricting, Republicans have control of drawing the maps impacting 187 congressional seats as opposed to the 84 seats Democrats will draw (the rest are drawn by independent panels). Even though Democrats control the House at the start of the decade, the power of Republicans to redraw the maps will make it difficult for them to hold on to the House throughout the 2020s. If we look at North Carolina where the presidential vote was a close split in 2020, with Trump carrying the state with 1.3 percentage points, Republicans voted on a map that gives them an advantage in ten of the fourteen congressional districts.[61] Any well-drawn redistricting map outweighs the will of the people, especially if the people are of color. As of this writing, with two-thirds of the congressional district lines redrawn, less than forty out of 435 districts will be considered competitive based on the 2020 presidential election results. Ten years ago, there were seventy-three competitive districts.[62]

Voter identification, especially since the selling of the Big Lie, has become a main tactic employed to suppress voters of color, being that they disproportionately lack drivers' licenses. Requesting some form of identification, on the surface, may not necessarily sound like a bad idea. However, a study released in 2017 when thirty-four states had some form of ID restriction (prior to 2006 no state required such identification) showed that those states with strict identification laws negatively impacted turnout within racial and ethnic minorities in both primary and general elections—with Latinxs being most negatively affected. Additionally, such laws skew voting to the political right. This has led former US Attorney General Eric Holder to equate strict voter ID requirements to a poll tax.[63]

One of the problems associated with strict voter identification has not actually been showing the ID but obtaining the identification. Studies indicate that hurdles to voting—large or small—substantially depress turnout.[64] One such hurdle has been implemented in Alabama, which requires state-issued IDs to vote. However, to make it harder for people of color to obtain a state-issued ID, the state shut down, in 2016, thirty-one driver license offices in predominately low-income neighborhoods, neighborhoods that are primarily of color.[65] Demanding an identification card, then making it difficult to obtain one, is an excellent example of how structural racism operates.

Purging voting rolls is another effective way of keeping people from voting. Most won't learn they've been purged until they attempt to vote. Targeting people in large metropolitan areas that lean Democratic is expected in states where Republicans control the process, places like Florida, Texas, and Ohio. For example, the metropolitan centers in Ohio targeted prior to the 2016 election (Cleveland, Cincinnati, and Columbus) had about twice the rates of Democrats than Republicans. At least 144,000 voters were removed from the rolls of these cities.[66] By 2019, Ohio sought to purge 235,000 voters for failing to vote in previous elections—the "use it or lose it" rule. Among those on the list was Jen Miller, director of the League of Women Voters who voted three times in the previous year. Also unexplained were some 20,000 voters from Franklin County, a Democratic stronghold. After a careful analysis of the names on the list, it was discovered that almost one in five names should not have been purged.

Purging voters, especially voters of color, can throw an election. Consider the 2018 gubernatorial race in Georgia. Democrat Stacy Abrams lost to Republican Brian Kemp by 55,000 votes. A year before the election, Kemp, who was

the Secretary of State, purged 500,000 voters from the rolls.
That same year the Governor signed the "exact match law,"
which empowered Kemp to throw out voter registration
forms whose information did not exactly match existing
state records. This allowed the Secretary of State to hold up
53,000 voter registrations for minor mismatches like a miss-
ing hyphen or a misplaced comma.[67] Also consider Wisconsin. Heading into the 2020 election, approximately 232,000
voters were on a state list identified for purging. Remember,
Trump won the state in 2016 by just 22,748 votes, less than
1 percent of the total vote cast. Checking the zip codes of
where those targeted to be purged lived, it was discovered
they came from predominately Black neighborhoods and areas populated by students—two groups that lean Democratic.
Those purged represented twice the number of Euroamerican voters even though they disproportionately represent
a smaller segment of the population.[68] Overall, from 2016
through 2019, seventeen million people were purged from
the voter rolls! And while there were names that needed to be
purged due to deaths or leaving the state, the overwhelming
evidence shows purging has been weaponized to keep voters,
predominately voters of color, from voting.

Besides purging voters an attempt exists to simply deny
voice to those who committed crimes earlier in life. In 2020,
5.17 million Americans lost the right to vote because they
were convicted felons, even after paying their debt to so-

ciety. Due to the prison industrial complex, one in sixteen African Americans are negatively impacted (3.7 times more than non-Blacks) and two percent of the Latinx voting population. Conservative estimates are that over 560,000 are disenfranchised—conservative because states unevenly report the ethnicity of prison populations.[69] When the voters of one of those states, Florida, passed a 2018 ballot referendum restoring voting rights to former felons, the Republican-controlled legislature passed a bill delaying full voting rights until they repay the state any and all court-ordered monetary sanctions while not enacting a procedure by which to inform former felons the amount due and how to satisfy the debt. Some 1.1 million former felons remain banned from voting.[70]

Poll watchers continue to be part of a long US history of intimidating voters of color and harassing election workers. Consider the made up "National Ballot Security Task Force," a brainchild of the Republican National Committee. They hired two hundred off-duty police officers and private security guards who, equipped with fake armbands, visible firearms, and official-looking walkie-talkies, participated in a bitter 1981 New Jersey governor's race by invading Democrat-leaning Black and Latinx polling sites. Those waiting to vote were turned away by the so-called officers. Some Latinx were literally chased away. The tactic seemed to have worked because the Republican candidate, Tom Kean, won the election by 1,800 votes. Democrats sued, and the case was settled out of court in 1982 with the RNC pledging to abstain from future poll watching unless they obtain prior court approval. These restrictions were lifted in 2018 when the RNC persuaded a federal judge that the Republicans can now be trusted not to return to the dirty tricks implemented in New Jersey some forty years earlier.[71]

As of this writing, training is being conducted by the Harris County Texas Republican Party in preparation for the 2022 midterm elections. Selling the Big Lie that fraud is occurring in densely populated Black, Latinx, and Asian-American Houston neighborhoods, the precinct chair of a northeastern suburban white neighborhood is recruiting white poll watchers "to have the confidence and courage" to inundate precincts comprised mainly by voters of color. This Jim and Jane Crow tactic was on full display in 2020 where at least forty-four incidents were reported of inappropriate behavior by poll watchers in Harris County. One nonpartisan election official, Cindy Wilson, reported that "two Poll watchers stood close to the black voters (less than 3 feet) and engaged in what I describe as intimidating behavior."[72]

Early voting has successfully increased election participation throughout the nation. This is bad news if the goal is to suppress the participation of people of color. So, in the name of fighting imaginary voter fraud, a 2012 law limiting early voting in Florida led to long lines, specifically in neighborhoods of color, dissuading many from casting their ballot. After the election, then-Florida Republican chairman, Jim Greer, who been attending strategy meetings since 2009 to implement this law, had no qualms admitting that his party sought to limit early voting for the sole purpose of suppressing the vote. "The Republican Party, the strategists, the consultants, they firmly believe that early voting is bad for Republican Party candidates," he said. "We've got to cut down on early voting because early voting is not good for us." As for the reason given to enact the law: protect voter integrity. He continued, "[the strategists and consultants] never came in to see me and tell me we had a (voter) fraud issue. It's all a marketing ploy."[73]

The threat Republicans seek to limit is Blacks voting, en masse, after church; a ritual affectionally known as "souls to the polls." Take Georgia as an example. During early voting, worshippers would pile into church vans after services and head to the polls to participate in democracy. The response to this threat is banning Sunday voting as of March 2021— three months after Georgia narrowly sent two Democrats to the Senate—one Jewish and the other Black—thus flipping the Senate. The ninety-eight-page document signed into law makes it difficult for Blacks to vote in future elections, while simultaneously making it easier for Euroamericans to vote by expanding early voting access in smaller, more rural counties.[74]

Another effective form of early voting is through mail-in ballots. During the 2020 presidential election, almost half of all votes cast were by absentee ballot, making the mass voting by mail experiment a success in democratic participation.[75] Nevertheless, this process has been attacked by Republicans under the false and unproven assertion that mail-in ballots are riddled with fraud. And yet, every so often, the disingenuous mask worn by politicians slips, allowing all of us to see the hypocrisy behind the rhetoric demanding electoral integrity. When Congressional Democrats proposed prior to the 2020 election $400 million to expand mail-in balloting amid the coronavirus pandemic, then-President Trump, in a refreshing moment of honesty during a live call-in to *Fox & Friends*, responded that if the bill is enacted, it would lead to "levels of voting that, if you ever agreed to it, you'd never have a Republican elected in this country again."[76] Congressman Matt Gaetz (R-FL) concurs. During an appearance on *Lou Dobbs Tonight*, Gaetz explained, "If we accept this universal mail-out balloting to people who didn't even request ballots, I don't think Republicans will ever win another national election again. That's why we have to stand and fight now."[77]

Limiting mail-in ballots is not enough. Drop-off boxes, especially in communities of color, must be limited. Also, the agency responsible for delivering the ballots must be destroyed. Nothing is off the table when it comes to suppressing the voice of communities of color from politically being heard. No institution is safe when it comes to maintaining political power. During the 2020 election, Trump pushed to defund the Post Office to limit the mail-in vote. Again, in a moment of non-spin honesty, he explained why he sought to slash funding for the Post Office. "They need that money in order to make the post office work, so it can take all of these millions and millions of ballots," Trump rationalized. "If we don't make a deal . . . that means they can't have universal mail-in voting."[78]

Texas provides a recent example of suppressing mail-in voting. New laws enacted during the 2021 legislative session demonstrate the effectiveness of suppression during the first election held since the 2020 presidential election. Of the more than 18,000 mail-in ballots cast during the state's March 2022 primary, the ballots of African Americans were disproportionately rejected. In Harris County, which includes Houston, Blacks were 44 percent more likely to have their ballots rejected when compared to Euroamericans in heavily white areas. The rejection rate of ballots went from 1 percent state-wide in 2020 to 15 percent in urban counties.[79]

Changing rules on how elections are called is probably the most dangerous outcome of the Big Lie. Political loyalists of the wannabe autocrat can be appointed to "ensure" the integrity of future elections. Trump failed to remain in office because of the safeguards in place to protect the integrity of the process by making it difficult to dismiss the electoral results. Secretaries of State and state legislators were powerless in 2020 in overturning the election results and appointing a slate of electors contrary to the will of the people. So, in 2021, legislators from fourteen states enacted laws to empower Republican state officials to take control of county election boards, thus eliminating such roadblocks, especially in states where Trump narrowly lost (Arizona, Georgia, Michigan, Wisconsin, and Pennsylvania). Other states (Texas and Florida) are following this lead. As of this writing, Republican officials are able in at least one state to overturn legitimate election results if they cite—without any need to prove—election fraud. No doubt other states will follow this lead.

The singular domestic policy of the Republican Party has become election-subversion legislation that strips independent election officials of their duties, replacing them with party hacks. Subversion strategies to weaken democratic guardrails have been legislated, designed to shift authority from election administrators to partisan politicians, even threating election officials with felony prosecution. To complicate matters, a concerted effort exists to recruit believers and advocates of the Big Lie to run for the post of Secretary of State throughout the country. As of this writing, twenty-one candidates who disputed the results of the 2020 election are running in eighteen states. And while many are running in solidly Red states, some are running in the battleground states of Michigan, Arizona, and Nevada, while others are running in the Bluer states of Colorado and California.[80] This may very well be the start of a trend to elect wolves to watch over the hen house.

Pushback from Democrats has been nonexistent as they sit on their hands unable to pass comprehensive voting rights. Preserving the Senate's filibuster—an anti-civil rights parliamentary procedure—is of greater importance than protecting the voting rights of historically minoritized communities. And even if after this book is published the Senate passes either the Freedom to Vote Act or the John Lewis Voting Rights Advancement Act, which would curtail the most outlandish voting suppression tactics listed above, the fact remains that the speed and ease it took to restrict and silence the voices of voters of color only indicates that when it comes to basic rights, whatever Euroamericans giveth, Euroamericans can taketh.

Rejecting Patriotism

What would eventually become the United States started as an apartheid republic where only white male landholders could vote. As time unfolded, more groups obtained legal status to participate in a more democratic political system.

This utopian dream of a democracy with liberty and justice for all caught the imagination of so many who for so long have been relegated to the margins of US society because of their race, their ethnicity, their gender, or their orientation. Advances in democracies were often paid with the blood of those seeking to live into the rhetorical promise of America, blood spilled in places like the Edmund Pettus Bridge or the grape fields of California. However, what seemed as a promise to those historically denied basic rights was interpreted as a threat to those whom the body politic was originally designed to unjustly and unfairly privilege.

From the mouths of Eurochristians flows flowery rhetoric calling for *brother*hood among all believers, but their hearts believe something utterly different. Justice and equality are fine, as long as it does not threaten their unearned power, profit, and privilege. And if it does, then unmerciful repression is required. Hence Eurochristianity becomes the great justifier of apartheid. This Eurochristian apartheid makes their interpretation of the message of Christ the greatest threat not only to communities of color, not only to those Eurochristians seeking to refute their complicity with white supremacy, but also to the whole of humanity regardless of faith affiliation, or lack thereof. Why? Because the fusing of Euro with Christianity to get Eurochristianity confuses unjust political systems with the will of God. Before Trump ever made that fateful ride down the escalator, the idea of MAGA, in sycophants' minds, was already a synonym for WWJD.

Changing demographics threaten the apartheid that was normalized and legitimized within US society under the rhetoric of democracy. America finds itself today torn asunder between two dominant worldviews: one that seeks to live into the ideal of democratic rule and the other that seeks to continue an apartheid that privileges the supremacy of Eurochristians. In short, America exists in the space between a reality based on democratic principles where $2 + 2 = 4$, and alternative facts of white supremacy where $2 + 2 = 5$. Unsurprisingly, a whitelash establishing a Jim and Jane Crow 2.0, undergirded by voter suppression that seeks to return to the original intent of the country's founding fathers, is currently unfolding as the response to those on the margins seeking the illusion of the American dream. To be a patriot today is to support through voter suppression the determination of political and economic policies by Euromales of means.

It is one thing to hold different political and religious positions, quite another to live in two different realities. A nation that does not share a common worldview is doomed to be ripped apart, fighting tooth and nail to see which vision will serve as its guiding light. The problem with the Eurochristian worldview—the real patriot's understanding of reality—is that it has historically been, and continues to be, detrimental to those with high levels of melanin. People of color should not assimilate as 2 + 2 = 5 Americans, for they will find themselves complicit with their self-harm. Following Eurocentric missionaries who hid colonialism in their Bibles is as deadly today as it was during first contact.

This chapter has been a call to become un-American, a call that requires being badass. Throughout these pages, a clarion call is given to refuse and reject how white supremacists have defined patriotism: a patriotism rooted in Manifest Destiny, Jim and Jane Crow, the Exclusion Acts, and Gunboat Diplomacy. The spiritual justification used for centuries of theft and genocide must come to an end. America is true to its history when it continues to advocate Eurochristian supremacy by calling it patriotism, and apartheid by calling it democracy. We who are not Euroamericans must hold these truths to be self-evident, that all humans—regardless of race, regardless of ethnicity, regardless of gender, regardless of orientation, regardless of ableness, regardless of documentation, regardless of faith tradition or lack thereof—are created equal, that they are endowed by their Creator with certain unalienable Rights, that among these are sustainable Life (healthcare rights), unrestricted responsible Liberty (voting rights), and the pursuit of Happiness (economic rights to the fruits of society). To be un-American is to embrace these truths unapologetically and

uncompromisingly. Any and all political or religious structures that refuse to bring these truths into reality remain
satanic and must not only be rejected, but (here is where the
badass is manifested) actively repudiated. It is not enough
to ignore, dismiss, ridicule, or reject the acts of patriotic
Euroamericans; they must be actively eliminated from the
body politic. The patriotism expressed by Euroamericans
for the past centuries have and continues to undermine the
democratic rhetoric they expound, regardless of whatever
sweet-sounding magniloquence they articulate.

But shouldn't we seek tolerance? some liberal-minded
Eurochristian might ask. No, there can never be tolerance
with death-causing patriotism. The liberative Good News
proclaimed by the Jesus of the Gospels of laying down one's
life for another has been pummelled to death by those demanding their Others to lay down their lives so the beneficiaries of Euroamerican supremacy can have life, and life
abundantly. For apartheid to reign, the rights and political
aspirations of communities of color must be kept in a choke-
hold. How can one be tolerant with ideologies responsible
for maintaining and sustaining structures of oppression?
There can be no tolerance with those who refuse to recognize the right of the disenfranchised to exist; there can be no
compromise with those who continue to pine for Euroamerican supremacy. To be badass is to reject white supremacy

and to make marginalized stories central in the retelling of the American experience. To be un-American is to overturn the tables of apartheid, chasing those profiting from our oppression out.

6

Playing the Prophet

Not long ago, I participated in an academic panel exploring the importance of the biblical text for our modern times. I was the only nonbiblical scholar on the panel (my discipline is social ethics), even though I've published more books dealing with the Scriptures than all the other Euroamerican panelists combined. At one point, one of the co-panelists referred to me as a prophet. I'm not sure if she meant it as a compliment, but I took it as an insult. I am not a prophet; I am a scholar. My work may be prophetic within the midst of the pathetic, but that does not mean it lacks academic rigor. By dismissing me as a prophet, these barely published lightweight scholars were able to maintain the illusion of their Euroamerican academic supremacy. Because I root my work in the life experiences of marginalized communities, specifically the Latinx experience, it simply cannot be as rigorous as what these Eurochristian navel-gazers define as academic excellence. How can a street rat from the slums of this nation, who could barely afford to go to a community college, compete intellectually with my co-panelists who graced the hallowed halls of the Ivies? If my writings can be dismissed as the ranting of an angry Latino, then the analytical critique I offer can also be dismissed—if not ridiculed as having no place within the academy.

Let's be clear, one reason why the scholarship of many from discarded communities is so cutting edge is because they refuse to docilely follow Eurocentric thought as if it is somehow superior to what is emerging from marginalized communities. Scholarship from the margins will always be superior to the dominant Eurocentric scholarship because it must be fluent in the writings of the dominant culture, as well as the wisdom from their own disenfranchised communities, a wisdom often ignored and dismissed by Euroamerican scholars. This is what liberative thinkers have called the "epistemological privilege" of the oppressed. Not that the oppressed are genetically smarter than their oppressors, but rather, because they must know everything oppressors know to survive in a Eurocentric-dominated world as well as everything within their own community. This provides them with a firmer grasp on reality than those who can survive without needing to know anything about the lives and experiences of those on their margins.

In the second book of this series, *Decolonizing Christianity*, my scholarship was heralded as prophetic by several reviewers. In that book I wrote: "If Trump is true to form, it is only a matter of time before he or his base voices threats of violence concerning the 2020 election."[1] Remember, this was published in April 2020, nine months before the Capitol insurrection. But in all honesty, there was nothing supernatural in making these so-called predictions. Anyone can predict the future when attention is given to the past. Peering into tomorrow is not as difficult as it may seem when one understands the past is constructed to justify the present, the launch pad for a desired trajectory into the future. The epistemological privilege of the marginalized provides a reliable context by which to read the signs of the times without the baggage of Eurocentric hope, so that a clearer picture of where we—as a society—are heading can be ascertained. Obviously, such a future is not determined. Scholarship that is prophetic arises in the land to warn that unless a change of course occurs, the destructive path we are currently on will come to pass. It does not take a clairvoyant to figure out that if we continue to ignore the ecological degradation of the environment, humanity will face a perilous future.

The purpose of divination is not to predict the future. Playing the prophet does not involve studying tea leaves or gazing at stars, but instead uses rigorous scholarship to study the current cultural and political milieu. With an eye on history, an ear to the daily newspaper, and a heart seeking faithfulness to one's moral compass, the scholar who is prophetic attempts to discern the future. "If white supremacy continues unabated," the scholar who is prophetic will say, "then we can expect to face certain particular challenges."

Being Prophetic

What good is the pursuit of the intellect if it does not contribute to the betterment of humanity? Eurocentric scholarship has been reduced to knowing, not transforming. For those who are minoritized by Eurocentric academics, the goal of the scholar who is prophetic is to seek harmony with what the future might bring while remaining faithful to one's beliefs and/or worldview—providing encouragement when it leads toward justice, dire warning when it does not. Unfortunately, a perusal of our daily newspapers makes the latter seem more normative than the former. This explains why those who were prophetic during biblical times ended up being thrown into wells, sawed in half, beheaded, chased out of town. Today they are denied tenure or simply not hired, academically blocked by Euroamerican scholars who will seldom measure up to the contributions being made by those they dismiss as activists and not true scholars. The scholar who is prophetic is either engaging in a foolish act or an act of courage. Not sure if I am being foolish or courageous, I will conclude this book by boldly turning my gaze to the future, and depending on my "predictions," seek necessary praxis if we desire a course correction.

I am neither a fortuneteller nor a soothsayer. I lack divination powers. I am no child of Orula. Again, I am a scholar—not a prophet—who nevertheless can read the signs, a skill anyone with a minimum education can cultivate. Choosing to play the prophet is a tradition as old as the biblical text. The books in the Hebrew Bible attributed to the prophets have a common thread that runs through all of them: *tsedeq*—justice. Prophets arose when injustices flourished. Their message was simple. One can never have a right relationship with one's God if *tsedeq* does not exist within society. They looked at the injustices of the present and then exclaimed that if a course-correction does not materialize soon, the people can expect death and destruction. As this book (and the two earlier ones of the series) has demonstrated, the United States, from the perspective of the marginalized, lacks *tsedeq*; ergo, it does not know God. If America continues its present course of insisting $2 + 2 = 5$, of insisting racism does not exist, of insisting climate change is a hoax, of insisting Q is truth, of insisting Trump is called and ordained by God, then it does not take a psychic to predict America is doomed.

If my reading of the signs is correct, then I can ascertain that the future being faced will become more deadly for US communities of color. The overt violence experienced by non-Euroamericans throughout most of US history up to the civil rights era was mostly replaced with institutional violence. In an attempt to mask the very visible violence that established Eurochristian superiority, violence was domesticated so that the structures—as opposed to individual bigots—enforced the white supremacist status quo. The noose may have been an effective means of sustaining an apartheid political structure, but the rhetoric of being the so-called greatest democracy on earth, the leader of the free world, became too incongruent with the reality faced by those who fell short of whiteness. Laws replaced nooses as a means of keeping people of color away from the polls while distancing Euroamericans from physical violence. Clear, unapologetic racist language employed in the past to justify suppression was replaced with polite race-neutral language that misappropriates Martin Luther King Jr.'s comment concerning not being judged by the color of one's skin but by the content of one's character. Political correctness in speech masks Euroamerican race-based intentions.

What I ascertain faces communities of color (truly hoping I am wrong) is frightful. If we consider the terror of the past that was required to forge a Eurochristian America, and if we consider the emerging terror of the present as demonstrated on January 6th, then we can expect that as whites seemingly become a minority, they will turn to greater violence to maintain their apartheid privilege. The insurrection was simply a disorganized dress rehearsal for what can become a more streamlined attempted coup during future elections. The insurrection was no fluke, but a carefully orchestrated first violent volley in a process to reestablish an apartheid America. The choice faced—probably for the first time—is if we will become a country where every citizen has an equal voice and vote in determining who will be entrusted with leading this fragile democracy, or if a theocracy will be imposed that merges the will of God with the will of Euroamericans. And while a slow-footed Trumpish coup fell short, the response to the Big Lie, in the form of voter suppression, is bringing an end to any minimal advances people of color might have made over the past half century.

When legislation fails to maintain apartheid, the next step for Euroamericans, fearful of losing their elevated space in society, is violence. This is the violence that echoes with the bombing of little girls attending a Sunday School class, the violence that places children in cages on our southwestern borders, the violence that snatches children from their parents and forces them into schools designed to erase their identity. When laws fail to safeguard Euroamericans' unearned power, privilege, and profit, we can expect a return to the noose. The kinder and gentler sophisticated technological lynching of a people that required a minimum of bloodshed because death came in the form of economics and political disenfranchisement will have to return with a more physical response if it hopes to be more effective in keeping us so-called barbarians at the gates.

Let's Go, Brandon

While an NBC sports reporter interviewed Brandon Brown after he won a NASCAR race in Alabama in early October 2021, a crowd in the background could be heard chanting "Fuck Joe Biden." Either mishearing or attempting to mask the vulgarity for national television, the reporter commented, "As you can hear the chant in the crowd: 'Let's go, Brandon.'" And hence was born a PG-rated version for white rage. "Let's go, Brandon" has appeared on T-shirts and face masks. A pilot on a Southwest flight from Houston to Albuquerque ended his greeting to passengers with "Let's go, Brandon," as did Representative Bill Posey (R-FL) on the House floor.[2]

Civility, as thin of a veneer that it was, has been long dead and buried in US political discourse. Some, myself included, trace this move toward hyper-incivility to 1995 when Newt Gingrich (R-GA) became Speaker of the House and, as previously mentioned, turned partisan politics into a bare-knuckle blood sport where winning elections at whatever the cost—even if it meant shutting down the government—wrecked the traditions of Congress. Today, clashes of differing ideas have been replaced with bullying and intimidation. Expletive-laden death threats have become the norm. Conservative congressman Fred Upton (R-MI) experienced this new white-rage norm. He has been receiving threatening voicemails since voting for a $1.2 trillion bipartisan infrastructure bill, proving the wolves will eat their own if one dares to step out of line. "I hope you die," began the anonymous voicemail, "I hope everyone in your fucking family dies . . . [you] fucking piece of shit traitor."[3] To put the necessities of the country first—a country that for decades has been in desperate need of updating its decaying infrastructure—is perceived as traitorous if it gives Democrats a political win. The hell with the political common good; more important is scoring partisan points.

The dominant Euroamerican culture, and the spiritual cover provided by Eurochristianity, is more than being able to say, "Fuck Joe Biden." They are demonstrating a will to power that reveals an attitude that can best be described as a "Fuck you America." Unless America is made great again by returning to the pre-civil rights era of white supremacy, all is perceived lost. Nostalgia has captured the imagination of some Euroamericans for that mystical time when there was no Black Lives Matter, when homosexuals remained neatly closeted, when police acted with deadly impunity, where a women's place was in the kitchen, where incels didn't exist because any woman was available for the taking, and where every seat from the classroom to the boardroom was reserved for Euromales due to white affirmative action. The America of the "Let's go, Brandon" crowd is one where centuries of Euroamerican brutality and vulgarity have sought to condition the oppressed to lick the hand of their oppressors in gratitude for the crumbs that would fall from the table their labor and resources set.

Communities relegated to reside under the master's table, which have for centuries experienced white rage, have been taught to be the wardens of their own panopticon. The "fuck you," cried out by Euroamericans, laid the foundation for a technology of discipline that had been successfully employed to condition people of color to self-restrain, a strategy designed to bureaucratically impose an internal police-state terror. Lynching the one creates the necessary fear needed for everyone else witnessing the lynching to respond through a self-imposed self-discipline—in the hope of avoiding a similar fate. Again, it does not take a prophet to see the rise of this white rage and not see the triumph of hatred over love because the former has always been more prevalent throughout US history. While we do not know if Biden will be reelected in 2024, even if he is, America will remain fucked because he will remain a reprieve to the insanity of our current political milieu.

Prophesying a Failing Democracy

Democracies die. No guarantee exists of its eternalness. No nation is immune to autocrats seeking to subvert the will of the people. Each new generation is tasked with its preservation. And this generation is failing miserably. Modern examples of democracies' demise occur when white nationalist parties capture positions in governments and exploit the power that comes with these positions to dismantle constitutional safeguards to rig future elections. Think of Russia, Hungry, Poland, Serbia. Outward forms of democracies—like elections—exist to mask autocrats' dictatorial rule as they designate opponents as traitors deserving silencing. And if elections go wrong as people vote against the usurpers of democracies, then elections are deemed to have been won through fraud, providing a righteous excuse to overthrow the election either legislatively (suppression of votes and transferring authorities to declare election winners to party hacks) or through violent insurrection (January 6th).

We are left wondering if America is even possible when one of the two political parties has discarded any shred of belief in the democratic process, choosing instead a cultish devotion to a wannabe autocrat. And in this upside-down world we live in, I find myself expressing sympathy for the likes of congressperson Liz Cheney (R-WY)—a far-right-wing warmonger and anti-LGBTQI warrior—because she is among the few Republicans who demonstrated a profile in courage by standing up against the anti-democratic sentiments of Trump and his congressional devotees, and as a result has been paying the price.

The greatest threat to US democracy continues to be Eurochristians, specifically Euroamericans with guns and wet dreams of being victorious in some near-future race war. White legislative goals unable to be achieved through the ballot will instead be pursued through the bullet. Confusing democracy for white supremacy, Euroamericans commit themselves to fight tooth and nail to maintain their unearned privilege, power, and profit, by whatever means necessary. Even if it means overrunning the barricades surrounding the Capitol, attacking the very police force that has historically defended their place within white society, and storming the halls of democracy to violently overturn an election while professing they are true patriots. In their minds, those "uppity" people of color demanding that their lives do matter are seen as a threat because they have the audacity to vote during open and free elections. These interlopers to Euroamerican citizenship must be dealt with, once and for all if need be. Assault rifles and other weapons of mass destruction are stockpiled by Euroamericans in preparation for the coming zombie apocalypse popularized in many cinematic blockbusters; only for them, the fear is not the walking dead seeking to eat their brains, but non-Euroamericans seeking to take their place.

Unlike any civilized nation throughout the world, America is awash in guns. They justify being armed to the teeth not just with rifles, but also flame throwers, body armor, night-goggles, bulletproof vests, and survival kits, embracing some misconstrued interpretation of the Second Amendment. Some 2As read books like *The Anarchist Cookbook* to learn how to make homemade bombs. The Second Amendment's purpose is, and always has been, to insure Euroamericans had the necessary firepower to kill Indians so their lands could be stolen, to subjugate Africans on the plantation so their labor could be stolen, and to marginalize all people of color so their basic human rights can be stolen. Racing toward a race war propels a hording of assault rifles designed for military combat in preparation for the apocalyptic moment when some final solution can be found for those falling short of whiteness. It will happen again. It can happen here. The hatred toward non-Euroamericans has become fertile ground for a neo-Auschwitz.

The success of reestablishing an apartheid America is high because one of the two major political parties have come to represent just one constituency. While the Democratic Party have multiple, and at times conflicting constituents—unions, different communities of color, queer rights activists, environmentalists, etc.—the Republican Party has the luxury of catering to a cohesive monolithic group of Euroamericans, mainly due to skin pigmentation but also a growing number of people of color who are ontologically white. Because being Eurochristian has become an extension of being Euroamerican, any legislative challenges to the privileged status of Euroamericans, like the dismantling of white affirmative action, is interpreted as a threat to Eurochristians. Such perceived threats solicit a hyper-defensive reaction. Any perceived threat to Euroamericans' unearned status is experienced by Eurochristians as a demonic attack to the very core of their identity. A violent response is called for. But first, the central teaching of the gospel message—love—must be rejected.

Trump was once asked what favorite biblical verse informed his thinking. His rambling response indicates a radical shift from the teachings of Jesus, and the failure of Eurochristians to correct their candidate demonstrates how they too have moved away from the gospel. According to Trump, his favorite verse is "An eye for an eye . . . That's not a particularly nice thing. But you know, if you look at what's happening to our country . . . how people are taking advantage of us, and how they scoff at us and laugh at us. And they laugh at our face, and they're taking our jobs, they're taking our money, they're taking the health of our country. And we have to be very firm and have to be strong. And we can learn a lot from the Bible, that I can tell you."[4] Forgetting that Jesus is repudiating the "eye for an eye" revenge form of direct retributive justice found in Exodus (21:22-25) with a call to "turn the other cheek" in Matthew (5:38-39), Trump as a candidate understood Eurochristianity as taking violent vengeance on those "taking our jobs . . . our money . . . the health of the country." And who are "those" to whom Trump refers? They certainly are not Euroamericans.

Just to be sure the standard bearer of the Republican Party calls for smiting one's enemies is not misquoted, we can see how his son, Don Jr., understood his father's message. During a December 2021 gathering of young conservatives, Don Jr. warned, "We've turned the other cheek and I understand sort of the biblical reference—I understand the mentality—but it's gotten us nothing. OK? It's gotten us nothing while we've ceded ground in every major institution in our country."[5] Because the fundamental message of the gospel is to put the interest of the other before one's own, of loving one's enemies, of walking the extra mile, it makes a poor strategy to gain or usurp power. The message of Jesus is for the meek, the losers of the world. Christian teachings like forgiveness are for the weak, explaining why Trump claims he has never had to ask God for forgiveness.[6] The Eurochristianity the Trumps and their followers advocate is a hypermasculine form reminiscent of Crusades, Inquisitions, and Colonialism. This is the blood-soaked Christianity of dictators and autocrats who wrap the violent, undemocratic core of their ideology with the cross.

Just to be clear, being white is not the problem. Rather the ideology of whiteness is the problem—an ideology that has captured one of the political parties, where the once 1980s white-power fringes have captured the central levers of power. Several Republican congresspersons were elected by advocating Q conspiracies while party leaders, like Minority Leader Kevin McCarthy, lack the spine to defend democracy over and against them. Even though the leadership knows the Big Lie is just that, a lie, they stand pusillanimously before a minority constituency whose votes in primary elections are oversized, affording them the power to send provocateur careerists to Washington to replace party moderates whom they portray as RINOs.

Prophesying a Race War

Again, I hope my predictions are wrong. Unfortunately, it does not take a sibyl to realize that unless we, as a society, move away from the current prevailing white rage undergirded by a non-cheek-turning Christianity based on "an eye for an eye," politically violent incarcerations and assassinations may become the new norm employed in future elections whenever it appears that Euroamerican supremacists will lose. "Lock her up" can very easily become a reality rather than a rhetorical rally chant. If we do not change course, it seems obvious that there will not be a peaceful

2024 presidential election. And even if it is peaceful, unless we as a nation turn from Eurochristian nationalism, it is only a matter of time before elections will be peppered with violence. As new laws are being passed to silence intellectual freedom—like exploring critical race theory—a fear exists of institutionalizing the persecution (incarceration or assassination) of those deemed unpatriotic. Such a fear is not unfounded. Today, militias and white supremacist groups are well organized and well-armed, poised for political action. They have an oversize voice within a new Republican Party that is hostile to any resemblance of a multiracial, multiethnic democracy.

Eurochristians have repudiated the core principle of love by aligning themselves with right-wing voters who express in words and deeds a hostility toward people of color, putting the teachings of QAnon and the worship of Trump over the teachings of the gospel and the worship of God. A pandemic going into its third year, economic distress caused by the pandemic, disrupted global supply chains, QAnon conspiracy theories running amuck, belief in a stolen election, a president-inspired insurrection, guns, a rise in well-armed militias, a polarized political system, a legislative quest to delegitimize the electoral process by eliminating the safeguards of democracy, and an embrace of white supremacy are the ingredients contributing to an atmosphere that can witness a violent attempt to dissolve the Union.

Let's be clear. A race war is already raging every time a person of color is killed when pulled over by the police or thrown into an immigration camp for lacking documentation. This is a cold race war based on an institutionalized violence that is just as efficient as physical violence. It's just a matter of time before new laws are put in place that can lead to those deemed not American enough being dismissed from federal, state, or local government employment. We can expect the dismissal of tenured professors who have the audacity to teach history, especially if they insist on teaching from the perspectives of the margins. We can expect the revocation of those of us who are naturalized citizens on charges of being un-American. This fear is real for those who insist on pursuing truth and repudiating the dominating ignorance. But fear is not limited to economic loss; it can also entail the loss of freedom or of life. To be a person of color living within the United States is to live in a rogue nation that finds itself in a cold race war that decimates its citizens of color, to exist in a state of constant terror where at any moment one's life or livelihood can be taken or one's body abused.

This cold race war existed in the past as a nation was built on the backs of those who fell short of whiteness. At times it turned hot, like when land belonging to the indigenous people was stolen through their genocide. Then cold when those who survived this holocaust faced the terror of being relegated to reservations. Hot when the nation fought to bring an end to slavery that relied on the sweat and blood of Africans to create an economic system that enriched those in the South and in the North. And cold when those who survived enslavement were forced to face the terror of lynching associated with Jim and Jane Crow. Hot when Mexico was invaded and its borders crossed, cold when facing the terror of lynching throughout the Southwest because of *Juan y Juana Cuervo*.

To live under the shadow of state-sponsored terrorism is not some past historical event. Violence against people of color in this nation is not ebbing. From the death of George Floyd in May 2020 to the celebration of the birth of Christ in 2021, some 1,646 people have been killed by law enforcement, or about three people a day, despite nationwide protests. And while more officers are facing murder or manslaughter charges due to societal consciousness raising, convictions remain exceptionally rare.[7] To make matters worse, a 2021 data breach at a Eurochristian crowd-funding website—GiveSendGo—demonstrated the union of Eurochristianity and white supremacy when it revealed how police officers and public officials have made millions of dollars in donations for acquitted vigilante murderers like Kyle Rittenhouse, far-right activists and their causes, and fellow officers accused of murdering people of color. Some of these far-right-wing groups are banned from raising funds on other platforms. Among the benefactors of law enforcement generosity are the domestic terrorist group the Proud Boys.[8]

Thus, it is foolish to believe such cruelties toward communities of color are part of a less enlightened distant past. Since the Anti-Defamation League started tracking white supremacist propaganda, 2020 was the highest amount ever recorded, a near doubling since the previous year.[9] Increased propaganda is not only used for recruiting purposes, but also to normalize and legitimize hatred and domestic terrorism. Domestic terrorism maintains the economic goal of stealing from bodies of color their labor, talents, and resources for the common good of Euroamericans through the institutionalization of violence. This institutionalized terrorism continues every time a person of color is stopped by law enforcement for driving while not being white. This institutionalized terrorism impacts us from the moment we are born to the efforts of gaining an education or employment to how we die.

Terrorism is not limited to state sponsorship. Individuals can also do their part. Among the greatest threat to people of color is a Euroman with a gun seeking to make America great again. The fear of Euromen has been experienced by Sikhs at an Indianapolis Fed Ex, Asian women at an Atlanta massage parlor, Latinxs shopping at an El Paso Walmart, Blacks when pulled over, or Queers dancing at an Orlando disco. Since Charles Manson's grisly murderous rampage in the late 1960s, numerous incidents have occurred aiming to ignite a race war. More recently we have witnessed the 1995 bombing of the Oklahoma City federal building that killed 168 people (including nineteen children) hoping to incite a *Turner Diaries* dystopia. To be a person of color in the United States is to always be a walking target, a means by which a race war can be ignited.

This cold race war will continue to simmer because a portion of America wants to see their nation less diverse, making them supportive of the reigning terror that reduces the number of citizens of color. Another portion of America, being more progressive, may express dismay at policies designed to decimate non-Euroamericans; nevertheless, they remain complicit with apartheid policies presented as a kinder and gentler decimation. To maintain their reign of terror, right-wing groups have been collecting firearms since the Klan first rode into the night to terrorize Blacks. Today, some left-leaning groups and people of color are seeking to no longer be targets. They are starting to also arm themselves. But are more guns and instruments of death the answer? Are guns needed to bring about peace and reconciliation? We are sitting on a powder keg as those salivating for a hot race war—from the Proud Boys to the Boogaloo Bros—play with matches (the "Boog" in "Boogaloo" is the group's shorthand for race war). The question is not *if* a violent conflict will occur; the question is when.

Euroamericans lying in their political crib hear gentle lullabies sung by white supremacists versed in Eurocentric theologies and philosophies. These intoxicating sirens lure the unsuspecting to lifelong slumber designed not to question the prevailing power structures. Languishing in privilege does not prevent the introduction of fear, specifically the fear of losing their unearned place in society. Should we be surprised? And while its apocalyptic conclusion may not be the goal of the majority of Euroamericans, the January 6th insurrection shows it is the aspiration of a vocal and powerful minority supported by Euroamerican political leaders pandering for votes. We find ourselves in a nation racing toward reintroducing an apartheid system. We find ourselves racing toward turning this cold race war hot.

Goddamn Eurochristianity

Nothing strikes greater terror in my very being than being approached by a Euroamerican wearing a big smile and carrying an even bigger Bible under their arm, for I understand all too well that this sacred book is often but a prop that provides cover for the most brutal, savage, and primitive urges of colonialism. This holy book tucked under their arm has become irrelevant because of how they have read and interpreted its text, a reading captured by white supremacy ideologies of the past few centuries. To bow one's knees to this white Jesus, created in their image, is to bow one's knees to all Euroamericans. America is indeed a Christian nation if Christianity is understood to be the spiritual dimension of white supremacy. The evangelical quest has nothing to do with saving souls, but everything to do with expanding power by converting others—even people of color—into their own white image.

How then do you get Eurochristians who may have the best of intentions, who love their children and pet their dogs, to stop engaging in death-causing acts that are evil? What explains churchgoers participating in the January 6th insurrection? By seducing them into believing their actions are for a cause that is greater than themselves. Religions provide justification for acts contradictory to the basic tenets of decency and morality. No greater human violations have been done than those acts committed in the name of some God. Eurochristianity is a cult that has the answer to all questions while providing the comfort and security of herd mentality. Only cultish thinking can transform a people claiming to follow the Prince of Peace into one of the most violent groups on the face of the earth.

And yet, Eurochristianity is not so much a religious cult as it is a political cult whose purpose is to obscure the terror faced by people of color and justify the abuse they experience as God's will. The personality cults that create political obedience litter the twentieth century from the right and from the left. They all share as a common denominator a charismatic leader tasked, during chaotic and uncertain times, with uniting a people to a particular worldview. These authoritarian political leaders exert power and foster sheepish docility like recent religious cults that led people to ends that have had deadly consequences. The intersection of a white supremacy political worldview with Eurochristianity changes the traditional understanding of cults by eliminating the need of an authoritarian leader. True, leaders do arise from time to time to lead Eurochristianity, as did Trump with the full support of false prophets, but Trump was not *the* cult leader, he was simply ordained to temporarily guide the already transhistorical Eurochristian cult. This Euroamerican cult does not rest with the leadership of one narcissistic man living within a particular moment in US history. This Eurochristian cult is so comingled with white supremacist nationalism that God and country become one substance, *homoousios*. To be an American is to be complicit—either consciously or unconsciously—with the doctrine of white supremacy. Because this doctrine is woven into the fabric of nationalism, Euroamericans need not be overtly racist or ethnically discriminatory, for the social structures are racist and ethnically discriminatory for them. They can remain bleeding heart liberals and still benefit from oppressive structures based on ethnicity or race.

Eurochristianity's purpose, as a political cult, is not spiritual, except to provide a thin veneer to give the illusion of divine will. The main reason for the cult of Eurochristianity to exist is to provide a theological justification for political acts that would make Jesus vomit. Reality is suspended by cult members so that they can engage in unchristian acts. A white supremacy political ideology is developed, masquerading as a spiritual belief that soothes the troubled conscience of cult members as they come before their white God with hands soaked in the blood of indigenous people, the blood of the enslaved, and the blood of countries invaded to steal their cheap labor and natural resources. The Jesus who calls for unconditional love for one's neighbor, who insists the needs of others must come first, is replaced with a white muscular Jesus who justifies the spiritual superiority of Euroamericans, a Jesus who calls for an eye for an eye, not some namby-pamby turning of the other cheek.

From time to time an authoritarian leader, an antichrist if you will, might arise to lead this Eurochristian cult, becoming the focus of Eurochristian idolization. Beyond simply merely flawed humans, this unchristian political figure is proclaimed to be the anointed of God, a type of Jesus for the modern age. Think of religious leaders like Franklin Graham who said Trump was chosen by God,[10] or Pentecostal pastor Paula White who proclaimed that "to say no to President Trump would be saying no to God."[11] While 29 percent of white evangelicals like Graham believe Trump is anointed, 53 percent of Pentecostals like White believe—with a correlation that the more one attends church, the higher the likelihood of belief in Trump's anointing.[12] Antichrists like Trump will arise throughout different generations, but they are not needed for white supremacy to function. Eurochristianity is a cult that has lasted generations with cult leaders during certain eras and without cult leaders during others. Leaders are not essential because the structures themselves take the responsibility of inflicting institutional violence to preserve the spiritual purpose of Eurochristianity, which is to justify white supremacy. Whether it be Tulsa in 1921, or Washington, DC, in 2021, Euroamericans reserve for themselves the right to burn things down to the ground whenever people of color get uppity and create wealth or flex their political muscle to oust white supremacist politicians.

Centuries of white supremacy undergirding the American experiment have sufficiently equipped Eurochristianity to function without a gravitating figure. The spiritual manifestation of white supremacy through white theology pointing to a white God does not need a particular flesh and blood individual to lead. Trump becomes an aberration because he takes on the messianic mantle of Eurochristianity. Most cults are known because they designate a spiritual leader to rule. Think of Jim Jones or Marshall Applewhite. But unlike these more traditional cults, a democratization has now taken place, resulting in the privileges once assigned to one leader now being dispersed based mainly on members' loyalty to America and its state's religion, Eurochristianity. This religious cult has functioned successfully through a decentralized apparatus where multiple figures have arisen, at times in conflict or contradiction, to guide devotees. Think of Billy Graham and his son Franklin, Jerry Falwell and his son Junior, Pat Robertson, Jim Bakker, etc. These modern-day spokespersons for the cult speak as if they were speaking for God. They direct all reverence and adulation to the white God created in their image—at a profit.

What then is the appropriate response to an institutional violence that is decimating those who challenge inherit racism and ethnic discrimination upon which Eurochristianity flourishes? Although true that one needs not be profane to be profound, those relegated to the vulgarity of lives in service to white supremacy, as a means of survival, must approach what Euroamericans have designated as sacred with contempt and irreverence. Profanity is not employed to shock the reader, nor to mask a lack of analytical depth. Profanity becomes the outward expression of a people who for centuries have been defiled and debased. When one lives the obscenity of their children in cages, the indecency of having their women sterilized against their will or knowledge, the crudeness of having their men face the state terror of border patrol agents and police officers, of identifying Latinxs (along with all who fall short of whiteness) as an

impure, unconsecrated people—then maybe, the only rever-
ent response is to say in full possession of esoteric wisdom:
"¡Goddamn white supremacy and the Eurochristian nationalism that maintains and sustains its spiritualization!"

There can never be reconciliation with a spiritual ideology
whose major purpose for existence was, and continues to be,
the silencing at best—extermination at worst—of people of
color. The usage of the word "extermination" is not some hyperbole. It is no coincidence that during the Covid pandemic,
Brown and Black people were disproportionately more likely
to be hospitalized and die due to the virus than whites.[13] It is no
coincidence that during routine traffic stops for minor infrac-
tions, Black and Brown people are disproportionately more
likely to be stopped and fined than whites, and when stopped,
have a higher likelihood of being killed by law enforcement.[14]
It is no coincidence that the life expectancies of Brown and
Black people are disproportionately lower than whites.[15] The
decimation of people of color through institutionalized violence means there can be no compromise with those complicit
with their slaughter, unless Euroamericans become saved by
renouncing and rejecting their white God and bow the knees
before the God of the disregarded, the God of the disenfranchised, the God of the dispossessed, the God who exists on
the margins of society regardless if there is or is not a God.

The question should never be if God exists, but what is
the character of this God that the community claims exists.

Euroamerican history has proven that the character of their God is that of a sadistic genocidal murderer. One need only to peruse the mountains of corpses, the remains of communities of color, sacrificed at the altar of this white God to satisfy *his* bloody thirst so that in return *he* can make America great. Maybe one day the wolf will dwell with the lamb, the leopard lie down with the goat, the calf and the lion will live together (Isa. 11:6), but until that messianic day arrives, those of us who are lambs, goats, and calves must try to get as far away as possible from devouring wolves, leopards, and lions whose love for us is reduced to an afternoon snack. There can be no reconciliation with those seeking to devour us, for they have no desire to give up the privilege of feasting upon whomever they yearn for. Just as predators will likely not choose to become vegans, so too will it be difficult for those whom white supremacy privileges to forsake their status to create some messianic kingdom, willingly abdicating the power they consider to be their birthright. Easier it would be to thread a camel through the eye of a needle.

Bipartisanship works best for white people. When Euroamerican conservatives and liberals find common ground through compromises, it often seems to be at the expense of people of color. Whiteness will always trump the need for radical change in any quest for a more just social order. Reconciliation is always damning for those who are not in the room where it happens. There can never be reconciliation when one party denies their Other's right to exist. When one party defines their Other as some simpleton or Marxist. A meeting of the minds will never occur with those who seek and desire our invisibility, if not our elimination. Hence, a prophet is not needed to foretell that before us lies a future of battle, a future of death and destruction, a future of decimation led by nationalist Eurochristians. We who are relegated to the underside of whiteness must thus wrestle with what our response is to a future where the followers of this white Jesus want what they have always achieved throughout history—our disappearance. The white Jesus leads to death, destruction, and damnation. Only the Black Jesus, or the Latinx Jesús, or the queer Jesus, or any other Jesus emerging from the underside of whiteness, has the cosmic power to save and liberate Eurochristians. Euroamericans, for the sake of their own salvation and liberation, must follow the Jesus of the disenfranchised. To stay clinging to the white Jesus would only bring forth more death.

Why? Because God takes sides. God chooses to stand in solidarity with those being oppressed, those being crucified on the crosses of racism, ethnic discrimination, heterosexism, classism, and sexism. This means that whoever God is, God sides with those being oppressed. Not because the oppressed are better, or wiser, or holier, but simply because they are being abused. These are "the least of my people," Jesus in the here and now; for Christ can always be found residing among those who are suffering oppression, who live in want, whose companion is misery. To stand with the oppressed is to stand against structures and people responsible for the oppression. These structures of oppression disguised as Eurochristianity will experience the wrath of God, God's damnation. Hence, I say it again: Goddamn Eurochristianity.

To stand with God is to join God's stance against oppression. Followers of the Divine are called and compelled to do likewise. God can never be a blond-haired Euroamerican because the biblical witness of God is of one who takes sides with those who are oppressed against their oppressors. Today, it is those relegated to the margins due to race or ethnicity who are the ones being oppressed, the ones who suffer hunger, thirst, nakedness, alienation, affliction, and incarceration. Unless . . . unless, people of color, struggling to decolonize their mind by rejecting Eurochristianity, come forth and become the change required for such a time as this, we will reap the Apartheid America being constructed before our very eyes. To be an imitator of Christ is to become a badass willing to share each other's pains, to share each other's sufferings, and together, share those pains and sufferings with the one who reminds us of the trials and tribulations of this world. A God who does not call us to build God's reign of justice or to seek liberation from all forms of sins, regardless of the cost to our personhood, is a false God better off damned for all eternity. When I die and stand before the throne of justice, if I find the white racist God worshipped by Euroamericans sitting on the throne, I would curse such a God and willingly choose to be cut off from any apartheid Heaven such a God has created.

All You Need Is Love

Many who have struggled for liberation remind us that wherever oppression exists, there is resistance. But how exactly does one resist without getting slaughtered? When one side controls the means of production, the ability to frame the worldview, and the backing of the police state, resistance may seem futile and could easily lead to annihilation. Complicating the call to resist is the Eurochristian demand to be good Christians who forgive and forget. But how can those suffering the PTSD of institutional violence break bread with those demanding an apartheid tomorrow through the suppressing of their voices and vote today? Those perpetuating and benefiting from institutionalized violence have lost all moral authority to paternalistically instruct those on their margins on how to seek and achieve their own liberation. Simply stated, communities of color who have experienced the consequences of generational oppression cannot offer forgiveness, nor can those who have benefited from those same structures of oppression obtain redemption if the latter insist on embracing their whiteness.

Concepts like offering forgiveness and forging reconciliation are indeed noble acts to be practiced, but what if their pursuit leads to greater terror falling upon the heads of the marginalized? When there is no meeting of the minds, when there is no desire to work through differences to arrive at a more just social structure, when those who hold power and privilege have no desire to share with those dismissed as their inferior, how can those on the underside of society be expected to embrace and kiss their tormentors? When those whom society is designed to favor are bent on an apartheid response to any future social order through the continuous subjugation of the marginalized, then there can be no forgiveness, there can be no reconciliation, there can be no peace. Susan Bro, who lost her daughter to the violence of the Unite the Right rally in Charlottesville in 2017, warns the nation that "the rush to hug each other and sing 'Kumbaya' is not an effective strategy."[16] History teaches we simply can't just hug it out without assigning accountability and taking responsibility. Unity is but a symptom of justice, not the end goal.

We know all too well how such efforts to reconcile usually play out. A lull in violence may indeed ensue. But all it takes is one misspoken word, one unaverted glance, one act of defiance, to again be smacked down. The dominant Euroamerican culture, regardless of rhetoric calling for reconciliation, has neither the desire nor the will to truly seek establishing a justice-based society. For if they were to be successful in such an effort, it would mean the loss of their unearned privilege within society. Devotees of the cult of Eurochristianity never want to be of "one accord" with those they deem to be undeserving of belonging. Euroamericans prefer to simply embrace people of color in fraternity without sacrificing the prevailing institutionalized social structures that secure their status. And here is why healing the division, widened during the Trump years, is so damned hopeless. No historical example exists where those benefiting by how oppressive political policies are structured have ever willingly renounced their privilege for the sake of creating a more just society. Any advances made in the cause for justice were usually paid for in blood, specifically the blood of the dispossessed.

Can we come together, heal our divide, and learn how to live in peace without the prevailing racism and ethnic discrimination? Can the disenfranchised keep coming forward in good faith seeking to convince those who refuse to listen? Those who refuse to examine their own faith tradition that justifies all sorts of bloodletting? The responsibility in seeking a solution to deal with the violence existing in the nation-home occupied by different races, ethnicities, and faith traditions can never lie with those historically tormented, but with their tormentors. Salvation can only begin with the turning away from sin, with the repudiation and rejection of the cult of Eurochristianity, an act I fear most Euroamericans—even those who are not religious—are unwilling to make. Proof of an unwillingness to repent was demonstrated by Eurochristians during the 2020 election, in their refusal to rebut and renounce Trumpism. In disproportionate numbers they came out and voted for the one who effectively wrapped himself in the flag and cross. They voted for their Eurochristian nationalist beliefs and the unearned privileges flowing from said beliefs.

So, if reconciliation for now is off the table because those benefitting from the current social structures are unwilling to share, what then becomes the proper ethical response? As tempting as violence may appear to be, it is not the answer. I find myself in agreement with social activist César Chávez, who once said, "I am not a nonviolent man. I am a violent man who is trying to be nonviolent."[17] Those involved in something constructive refrain from violence, while those not committed to the rebuilding of a more just order tend to advocate the more destructive path of violence. Chávez insisted that nonviolence requires greater courage and militancy. Besides, on a more practical level, violence cannot be the answer because the dominant Euroamerican culture has control of all the weapons of mass destruction. Not just the vast nuclear arsenal, but the stockpiles of guns collected by Euroamericans in preparation for the coming apocalypse.

Eurochristian disciples of white supremacy possess the *imago Dei*, regardless of their complicity with oppressive structures. Touched with the spark of the Divine, they retain the ability to become followers and imitators of the God of the oppressed, and despite themselves, still have worth and dignity as humans. True, they fall short of humanity because of their complicity with barbaric and savage policies; still, they are capable of salvation from the sin of their white supremacy. How sad then that they choose to muzzle this God of the disenfranchised by giving voice to what makes them wretched. They may desire the good, but choose the wicked. Who will deliver them from their sinful nature? Through their racist actions and words, they have shut the door to the God of the oppressed who stands on the other side knocking.

The horrors Euroamericans inflict coupled with a refusal to embrace a saving grace can easily lead to hating them—hating them for what they say and what they do. But hate makes those whom they have disenfranchised like them. Hate, and the violence it unleashes, makes people of color no better than Euroamericans. They are not to be hated but instead pitied because their tight grasp on power has robbed them of their humanity and of the ability to call themselves the children of God. Although they can choose to walk humbly with their Creator, destined to dwell in the House of the Lord, they have chosen to mire in the mud with the demonic. How sad—how utterly sad. Demonstrating pity rather than hatred is a start, but not enough. We should be concerned with the liberation of Euroamericans, not so much for their sake, but if they turn away from their complicity with white supremacy, others within communities of color might be able to breathe a bit easier. But let's be clear, forsaking the use of violence does not mean violence is not present. The call is for the oppressed not to engage in violence for spiritual and practical reasons, but this does not ignore that violence is already being employed.

The prevailing violence has desensitized Euroamericans. Eurochristian nationalism lacks any understanding as to what love is, specifically unconditional love biblically referred to as *agapē*. The attempt by Eurochristians to use the concept of love as a virtue is highly problematic because their understanding of love is autocratic and paternalistic. One loves their racial and ethnic Other similarly to how one loves a dog. Dogs, not being equal to humans, must be supervised and cared for. And every so often, when a dog gets out of line, they require and deserve a swift kick to remind them of their place, remind them who is boss. True love, in their minds, should not spoil the beast, hence the rod can never be spared. Eurochristian love is tough love, complicit with domination and manifested through subjugation. *Agapē*, as taught in the gospel, is therefore incongruent with any manifestation of Eurochristianity. Yes, the words of love are articulated, but like a tree that produces no fruit, it is barren.

Any Eurochristian ethics based on love is thus doomed to fail. In his groundbreaking book, *Situation Ethics*, Euroamerican ethicist Joseph Fletcher argued that "the ruling norm of Christian decisions is love: nothing else."[18] Basing all moral reasoning on the universal Christian virtue of love, at first glance, may appear as an excellent methodology by which to determine praxis. But Fletcher assumes Euroamericans know what is love, know how to love. Unfortunately, a history of how they have shown love to those on their margins indicates they do not know the meaning of the word. For centuries Euroamericans have engaged in a history of white supremacist hatred—from genocide to slavery to suppression, inflicting terror with a clear conscience. How? By reclassifying that which is immoral as legal. Because Euroamericans do not know what love is and lack experience in implementing love, it becomes problematic to create an ethical paradigm based on how they understand and implement such a principle. Fletcher's simple formula is thus ill-fated.

For those of us who have been intoxicated with postmodernist thought, the idea of proposing a universal truth—any universal truth—becomes nauseating. And yet, maybe we are to blame for the rise of alternative facts and exaggerated truths. In rejecting all universalities, all perspectives become equal in the matrix of perspectives. The pronouncements of white supremacist groups like Oath Keepers or Proud Boys have equal moral value with those from Black Lives Matter or #MeToo. The reasoning for segregation as understood by the Klan, state's rights, is just as valid as the reason for desegregation offered by the civil rights movement. QAnon and the *New York Times* have equal weight. Such postmodern suspicion of truths justified a Trump whose lies were instead understood as truth. But can moral agency be employed without the ability of stating this is good and that is evil? If so, who decides? If basing an ethical paradigm on the subjectivity of those whom society is designed to benefit while presenting the philosophy undergirding said model as objective is problematic, then what becomes a more acceptable basis?

If there is to be a universal truth informing praxis—truth with a lower case "t"—then it cannot rely on definitions or experiences of those whom society privileges at the expense of Others. Only those who are harmed by structures of oppression have what liberative theologians call the epistemological privilege, the insight of knowing which groups due to race, class, gender, and orientation benefit or suffer by how society is constructed. Not all religious understandings concerning universalities are equals in the matrix of opinion, where the perspectives emerging from marginalized communities are but one of many competing interpretations.

How those on the underside of society understand reality takes priority over and against any Eurocentric perspectives. Not because the disenfranchised are holier, or smarter, or closer to God. Their perspectives are closer to whatever Truth might be because the oppressed occupy a space that gives them a better grasp of reality. With such an understanding, we can boldly claim Black Lives Matter is closer to justice and truth than the Proud Boys' worldview; not because BLM is perfect, but because they exist as a response to oppression. And as we already stated, God takes sides. So yes, God sides with Black Lives Matter over and against the Proud Boys!

The space occupied by US marginalized communities provides the ability of better understanding how social structures are designed to sustain their marginalization and know the arguments and excuses employed by Euroamericans to justify the oppressive structures designed to privilege them. If a gospel-based praxis, or a perspective derived from said praxis, is to be embraced, then Eurochristianity must first be rejected, for any claim to universality must arise from the social location of the marginalized, not Euroamericans, if any hope exists for validation. So, what is a possible common denominator shared by most—if not all—US disenfranchised communities? What is it that the oppressed want? At the very least, we can begin with the cry: "Stop killing us." "Stop oppressing us." "Let us live in peace and equity." "Stop being enriched off our labor, talents, and resources." In short: "Stop harming us." And maybe here—and not Fletcher's concept of love—is where our quest for the ruling norm of engaging in ethical practice is found. What does it mean to base ethical action not on the perpetrator's "love" but instead on the abusee's cry "don't harm me"?

We can look to the ancients who provide an excellent alternative to Fletcher's "love." One of the oldest documents serving as foundational in ethical thought is the Hippocratic Oath, a binding code for those who practiced the medical profession. And while these particular words do not actually appear within the original 245 BCE oath, it has come to be understood by three Latin words: *Primum non nocere*, better known as *first do no harm*. While suspicious of universal pronouncements, the dictum of doing no harm when it comes to engaging in praxis may be as close as we can get to a guiding universal principle on how best to respond to the terrorism faced by communities of color and as a strategy in battling against the forces bent on reimposing an apartheid political system.

No doubt the beneficiaries of apartheid will attempt to gaslight the abused by insisting they are the ones who are oppressed, they are the true victims. According to a Hill-HarrisX poll, 75 percent of Republicans, 55 percent of Independents, and 38 percent of Democrats believe white Americans are subject to discrimination.[19] "Don't Tread on

Me" becomes a smokescreen where claiming discrimination masks white privilege. Because those whom society privileges present themselves as victims, Euroamericans have lost all moral authority to say anything about anything when it comes to moral issues. We can always hope Euroamericans would learn the first ethical principle of doing no harm; but is it hopeless?

Ending on a Note of Hope?

The good news about prophecies is that they are not written in stone. Humans have the free will to change course. But this author fears the grip Eurochristianity has upon the souls of Euroamericans. Maybe salvation from the sins and evils of Eurochristianity might lead to a break with the expected as a new trajectory is mapped out. Unfortunately, I remain hopeless. "For as a dog returns to its vomit, so too do fools return to their folly" (Prov. 26:11). To embrace the hope that the oppressed will somehow avoid the reality of a death-causing America that is hostile to all who fall short of whiteness only reinforces one's complicity with their self-discipline.

A prophet is not needed to discern that America is at war with itself, a cold race war on the verge of turning hot. We are rushing to an Apartheid America, the result of a violent confrontation. I pray I am wrong. We are left asking if as a nation we are condemned to the consequences of the prevailing cult of Eurochristianity that continues to advance the failed policies of white supremacy. Is there any hope for those who for generations bowed their knees before the white Jesus of genocide, slavery, Manifest Destiny, gunboat diplomacy, colonialism, and all manner of oppressive political structures? Maybe the only hope is a badass attempt of being un-American by totally repudiating and rejecting Eurochristianity and the political and cultural symbols it signifies. To be un-American, as this book has argued, is a call to crucify what it means to be an American, so that a new creature can be born again. What is needed, if we wish to survive as a nation, is for Euroamericans to get "saved." Their salvation is made possible when they crucify their white supremacy, their white theology, and their white Jesus. Only by nailing all that provides them with unearned privilege to that cross can a semblance of resurrected hope arise.

Cognizant that anyone can demonstrate courage from a safe distance, I would hope that I would possess the courage to live for my beliefs without killing or oppressing for my beliefs. What is the point of faith in the absence of justice? The best way to be faithful to the God of liberation that may or may not exist (not that it really matters) is to fight for the liberation of Others. The best manifestation of worship is to exercise free will. The best way to be human is to un-shackle one's mind from theologies that reinforce servitude. And maybe in the final analysis, this is the true definition of what it is to be a badass Christian.

Notes

Chapter 1

1. Captain John Underhill, *Newes From America or, A New and Experimentall Discoverie of New England* (London: J. D. for Peter Cole, 1638), 40.

2. Benjamin Franklin, *Observations Concerning the Increase of Mankind, Peopling of Countries, &c.* (1755; repr., Boston: S. Kneeland, 1918), 224.

3. Noel Ignatiev, *How the Irish Became White* (New York: Routledge, 2009), 49.

4. Louise DeSalvo, "Color: White/Complexion: Dark," in *Are Italians White? How Race Is Made in America*, ed. Jennifer Guglielmo and Salvatore Saleerno (New York: Routledge, 2003), 28.

5. Linda So and Jason Szep, "Special Report: Reuters Unmask Trump Supporters Who Terrified U.S. Election Workers," Reuters, November 9, 2021.

6. "USCP Response to OIG Report #3," *United States Capitol Police Press Release*, May 7, 2021.

7. Lorenzo Ferrigno, "Donald Trump: Boston Beating Is 'Terrible,'" CNN, August 21, 2015.

8. Lisa Lerer, "Menace Grows Commonplace Among GOP," *New York Times*, November 12, 2021.

9. PPRI Staff, "Competing Visions of America: An Evolving Iden-

tity or a Culture Under Attack? Findings from the 2021 American Values Survey," Public Religion Research Institute, November 1, 2021.

10. Justin Nortey, "Most White Americans Who Regularly Attend Worship Services Voted for Trump in 2020," Pew Research Center, August 30, 2021.

11. Joe Walsh, "Report: U.S. Government Paid Over $2.5 Million to Trump's Businesses," *Forbes*, October 27, 2020.

12. Jessica Chasmar, "Van Jones Says, 'A Lot of Democrats' Are Hurting Right Now," *The Washington Times*, November 4, 2020.

13. Aamer Madhani, "Biden Declares 'America Is Back' in Welcome Words to Allies," Associated Press, February 19, 2021.

Chapter 2

1. Edmund S. Morgan, *American Slavery, American Freedom: The Ordeal of Colonial Virginia* (New York: W. W. Norton, 1975), 329–33.

2. Ronald Reagan, "Inaugural Address," Washington, DC, January 20, 1981.

3. Dan T. Carter, *From George Wallace to Newt Gingrich: Race in the Conservative Counterrevolution 1963–1994* (Baton Rouge: Louisiana State University Press, 1996), 64.

4. "Biden Lashes Out at Palin's 'Pro-America' Comment," CNN, October 17, 2008.

5. Alexandria Ocasio-Cortez (NY), Ilhan Omar (MN), Ayanna Pressley (MA), Rashida Tlaib (MI), Jamaal Bowman (NY), and Cori Bush (MO).

6. Chris Cameron, "In a Speech to a New Hampshire GOP Group, Pence Calls Systemic Racism a 'Left-Wing Myth,'" *The New York Times*, June 3, 2021.

7. Devan Cole, "Graham Denies Systemic Racism Exists in US and Says 'America's Not a Racist Country,'" CNN Politics, April 25, 2021.

8. Kimmy Yam, "Nikki Haley Claims 'America Is Not Racist,' Later Says She 'Faced Discrimination,'" NBC News, August 25, 2020.

9. Phillip M. Bailey, "'America Is Not a Racist Country,' Tim Scott Says in Republican Rebuttal to Biden's Speech," *USA Today*, April 28, 2021.

10. Jack Brewster, "Biden Says He Doesn't Think America Is Racist—But Slavery, Jim Crow 'Had A Cost,'" *Forbes*, April 30, 2021.

11. Cole, "Graham Denies Systemic Racism."

12. PRRI Staff, "Dueling Realities: Amid Multiple Crises, Trump and Biden Supporters See Different Priorities and Futures for the Nation," Public Religion Research Institute, October 19, 2020.

13. Unless otherwise cited, all biblical passages are translated by the author from the original Hebrew and/or Greek.

14. Kara Fox, Krystina Shveda, Natalie Croker, and Marco Chacon, "How US Gun Culture Stacks Up with the World," CNN, November 26, 2021.

15. Kara Fox et al., "US Gun Culture."

16. Katelyn Polantz, "In Capitol Riot Cases, Judges Split on Whether to Keep Defendants in Jail Before Trial," CNN, February 19, 2021; "Judge Says Trump's 'Steady Drumbeat' of the Big Lie Could Continue to Inspire His Supporters to Take Up Arms," CNN, May 27, 2021.

17. Jeffrey M. Jones, "U.S. Church Membership Falls Below Majority for First Time," Gallup, March 29, 2021.

18. Paul A. Djupe, Jacob R. Neiheisel, and Kimberly H. Conger, "Are the Politics of the Christian Right Linked to State Rates of the Nonreligious? The Importance of Salient Controversy," *Political Research Quarterly* 7, no. 4 (2018): 910.

Chapter 3

1. J. Jorge Klor de Alva, "Spiritual Conflict and Accommodation in New Spain: Toward a Typology of Aztec Response to Christianity," in *The Inca and Aztec States, 1400–1800: Anthropology and History*, ed. George A. Collier, I. Rosaldo Renato, and D. Wirth John (New York: Academic, 1982), 353.

2. Joseph R. Dodson, "The Fall of Men and the Lust of Women in

Seneca's *Epistle 95* and Paul's Letter to the Romans," *Novum Testamentum* 59 (2017): 355–56.

3. Pope Gregory, *Dialogues* 2.2, trans. Odo John Zimmerman, *The Fathers of the Church* 39 (New York: Fathers of the Church, 1959), 60.

4. Justin Martyr, *The First Apology* 21, in *St. Justin Martyr: The First and Second Apologies*, trans. Leslie William Barnard (Mahwah: Paulist Press, 1997), 38.

5. Peter Wehner, "Are Trump's Critics Demonically Possessed?," *The Atlantic*, November 25, 2019.

6. Meagan Flynn, "Trump's Spiritual Advisor Seeks His Protection from 'Demonic Networks' at Reelection Rally," *The Washington Post*, January 19, 2019.

7. Augustine, *The City of God*, book 2, chapter 2.

8. *The City of God*, book 5, chapter 1.

9. *The City of God*, book 14, chapter 28.

10. *The City of God*, book 15, chapter 4; book 19, chapter 17.

11. Origen, *Commentary on Matthew* 1.16.8. Emphasis added.

12. *Cur Deus Homo* 1.11–23.

13. *Commentary on Romans* 2.3.

14. Lewis E. Jones, "Power in the Blood" (1899).

15. Martin Luther, "Admonition to Peace: A Reply to the Twelve Articles of the Peasants in Swabia," *Luther's Works*, vol. 46, *The Christian in Society III*, ed. Robert C. Schultz (1525; Philadelphia: Fortress, 1967), 39.

16. Luther, "Admonition," 50.

17. Luther, "Admonition," 50.

18. John Calvin, *Institutes of the Christian Religion*, trans. John Allen (Philadelphia: Presbyterian Board of Publication, 1813), vol. 1, book II, chapter 1: V.

19. *Institutes*, vol. 1, book 1, general syllabus: IV.

20. *Institutes*, vol. 1, book 1, chapter 7: I.

21. *Institutes*, vol. 1, book 2, chapter 8: XIV.

22. *Institutes*, vol. 1, book 2, chapter 3: VI.

23. *Institutes*, vol. 1, book 2, chapter 3: XI.

24. Max Weber, *The Protestant Ethic and the Spirit of Capitalism*, trans. Talcott Parsons (New York: Charles Scribner's Sons, 1958), 98–139, 157–63, 175.

25. John O'Sullivan, "Annexation," *United States Magazine and Democratic Review* 17, no. 1 (July and August 1845): 5.

26. Exodus 23:23; Joshua 6:21.

27. Sydney E. Ahlstrom, *A Religious History of the American People* (New Haven: Yale University Press, 1972), 845, 877–78.

28. Ronald Takaki, *A Different Mirror: A History of Multicultural America* (Boston: Little, Brown, 1993), 191.

29. Robert F. Smith, *What Happened in Cuba? A Documentary History* (New York: Twayne, 1963), 85–87.

30. John C. Calhoun, *The Works of John C. Calhoun*, vol. 2 (Altenmünster, DE: Jazzybee Verlag, 2015 [1837]), 357.

31. Walter Rauschenbusch, *A Theology for the Social Gospel* (Nashville: Abingdon, 1917), 186.

32. Walter Rauschenbusch, *Christianizing the Social Order* (1912; New York: Macmillan, 1926), 376.

33. Walter Rauschenbusch, "The Contribution of Germany to the National Life of America," commencement address to Rochester Theological Seminary, 1902. Cited in Warren L. Vinz, *Pulpit Politics: Faces of American Protestant Nationalism in the Twentieth Century* (Albany: State University of New York Press, 1989), 1–2.

34. Walter Rauschenbusch, "The Church and Social Questions," in *Conservation of National Ideals* (New York: Fleming H. Revell Company, 1911), 106.

35. Walter Rauschenbusch, "The Belated Race and the Social Problem," lecture delivered before the American Missionary Association, 1912.

36. Rauschenbusch, *Christianizing the Social Order*, 278.

37. Rauschenbusch, "The Contribution of Germany to the National Life of America," 4.

38. Walter Rauschenbusch, "The Present and the Future" (1898), cited in Christopher H. Evans, *The Kingdom Is Always but Coming: A Life of Walter Rauschenbusch* (Grand Rapids: Eerdmans, 2004), 50–51.

39. Rauschenbusch, *Christianizing the Social Order*, 110.

40. Rauschenbusch, *Christianizing the Social Order*, 114–15.

41. David Brooks, "Obama, Gospel and Verse," *New York Times*, April 26, 2007.

42. Reinhold Niebuhr, "Anglo-Saxon Destiny and Responsibility," *Christianity and Crisis* 3, no. 16 (October 4, 1943): 2.

43. Reinhold Niebuhr, "Plans for World Reorganization," *Christianity and Crisis* 2, no. 17 (October 19, 1942): 3–6.

44. Reinhold Niebuhr, *Moral Man and Immoral Society: A Study in Ethics and Politics* (New York: Charles Scribner's Sons, 1932), 128.

45. Reinhold Niebuhr, *The Structure of Nations and Empires: A Study of the Recurring Patterns and Problems of the Political Order in Relationship to the Unique Problems of the Nuclear Age* (New York: Charles Scribner's Sons, 1959), 202.

46. Niebuhr, *Structure of Nations and Empires*, 22, 25, 38, 66, 203.

47. Josh Dawsey, "Trump Derides Protection for Immigrants from 'Shithole' Countries," *Washington Post*, January 12, 2018.

48. U.S. Census Bureau, https://www.census.gov/popclock/, accessed June 8, 2020.

49. World Population Balance, https://www.worldpopulationbalance.org/population_energy, accessed June 8, 2020.

50. Stanley Hauerwas, *The Peaceable Kingdom: A Primer in Christian Ethics* (Notre Dame: University of Notre Dame Press, 1983), 103.

51. Stanley Hauerwas, *After Christendom? How the Church Is to Behave if Freedom, Justice, and a Christian Nation Are Bad Ideas* (Nashville: Abingdon, 1991), 45.

52. Stanley Hauerwas, *A Community of Character: Toward a Constructive Christian Social Ethics* (Notre Dame: University of Notre Dame Press, 1981), 112.

53. Hauerwas, *A Community of Character*, 74.

54. Stanley Hauerwas, "The Gesture of a Truthful Story," *Theology Today* 42, no. 2 (July 1985): 185–86.

55. Stanley Hauerwas, *Wilderness Wanderings: Probing Twentieth-Century Theology and Philosophy* (Boulder, CO: Westview Press, 1997), 225–26.

56. Stanley Hauerwas, "Learning to See Red Wheelbarrows: On Vision and Relativism," *Journal of the American Academy of Religion* 45 (1977): 649.

57. Hauerwas, *A Community of Character*, 10.

58. Hauerwas, *The Peaceable Kingdom*, 107.

59. Bob Smietana, "Michael Flynn Calls for 'One Religion' at Event That Is a Who's Who of the New Christian Right," *Washington Post*, November 19, 2021.

60. Andrew Kaczynski and Nathan McDermott, "Trump's National Security Advisor Pick Regularly Pushed Sharia Law Conspiracy Theories in Speeches," CNN, November 23, 2016.

61. @JoshMandelOhio, November 13, 2021.

Chapter 4

1. Cybersecurity & Infrastructure Security Agency, "Joint Statement from Elections Infrastructure Government Coordinating Council & The Election Infrastructure Sector Coordinating Executive Committees," November 12, 2020, https://www.cisa.gov/news/2020/11/12/joint-statement-elections-infrastructure-government-coordinating-council-election.

2. Rob Kuznia, Curt Devine, Nelli Black, and Dre Griffin, "Stop the Steal's Massive Disinformation Campaign Connected to Roger Stone," CNN, November 14, 2020.

3. Ryan Nobles, Zachary Cohen, and Annie Grayer, "'We Control Them All': Donald Trump Jr. Texted Meadows Ideas for Overturning 2020 Election Before It was Called," CNN, April 9, 2022.

4. Alan Feuer, "Trump Campaign Knew Lawyer's Voting Ma-

chine Claims Were Baseless, Memo Shows," *New York Times*, September 21, 2021.

5. Stephen Collinson, "Trump's Big Lie Is Changing the Face of American Politics," CNN, September 16, 2021.

6. Maggie Astor, "Politicians Love Email, Where Lies Go Unpoliced," *New York Times*, December 14, 2021.

7. Stephen Collinson, "Bogus GOP Arizona Audit Confirms the Obvious: Biden Won," CNN, September 24, 2021.

8. Meryl Kornfield, "Why Hundreds of QAnon Supporters Showed Up in Dallas, Expecting JFK Jr.'s Return," *Washington Post*, November 2, 2021.

9. Tina Nguyen, "Trump Isn't Secretly Winking at QAnon. He's Retweeting Its Followers," Politico, July 12, 2020.

10. PRRI Staff, "Competing Visions of America: An Evolving Identity or a Culture Under Attack? Findings from the 2021 American Value Survey," Public Religion Research Institute, November 1, 2021.

11. Zachary Cohen, "China and Russia 'Weaponized' QAnon Conspiracy Around Time of US Capitol Attack, Report Says," CNN, April 19, 2021.

12. Davey Alba, "'Q' Has Been Silent, but QAnon Is Flourishing," *New York Times*, December 21, 2021.

13. United States Census, *Projecting Majority-Minority* (Washington, DC: US Department of Commerce, 2014).

14. Michael Wines and Mark Cramer, "Census Undercounted Latino, Black and Tribal Residents," *New York Times*, March 11, 2022. The census missed 4.99 of every 100 Latinxs, 5.64 of every 100 Native Americans, and 3.3 of every 100 African Americans while wrongly adding 1.64 to every 100 Euroamericans and 2.62 to every 100 Asian Americans.

15. Tucker Carlson, *Fox News Primetime*, April 8, 2021, https://video.foxnews.com/v/6247704505001.

16. Elizabeth Williamson, "How America Got to Charlottesville: An Expert Draws a Map," *New York Times*, November 3, 2021.

17. Steve Benen, "Republicans Become More Brazen about Embracing 'Replacement Theory,'" MSNBC, September 27, 2021.

18. Williamson, "How America Got to Charlottesville."

19. Robert A. Pape, "What an Analysis of 377 Americans Arrested or Charged in the Capitol Insurrection Tells Us," *Washington Post*, April 6, 2021.

20. Maureen A. Craig and Jennifer A. Richeson, "On the Precipice of a 'Majority-Minority' America: Perceived Status Threats from the Racial Demographic Shift Affects White America's Political Ideology," *Psychological Science* 25, no. 6 (2014): 1189–90.

21. Benjamin Franklin, *Observations Concerning the Increase of Mankind, Peopling of Countries, &c.* (1755; repr., Boston: S. Kneeland, 1918), 224.

22. "Kuban Ku Klux Klan Is Formed in Cuba," *Daily Clarion-Ledger* (Jackson, MS), September 22, 1928.

23. Frank Guridy, "'War in the Negro': Race and the Revolution of 1933," *Cuban Studies 40*, ed. Louis A. Pérez Jr. (Pittsburgh: University of Pittsburgh Press, 2010), 55.

24. John Blake, "White Supremacy with a Tan," CNN, September 4, 2021.

25. Aaron Zitner, "Hispanic Voters Now Evenly Split Between Parties, WSJ Poll Finds," *Wall Street Journal*, December 8, 2021.

26. Jonathan Vespa, Lauren Medina, and David M. Armstrong, "Demographic Turning Points for the United States: Population Projections for 2020 to 2060: Population Estimates and Projections," U.S. Census Bureau (Washington, DC: U.S. Department of Commerce, 2018), 7.

27. James Gangel et al., "'They're Not Going to F**king Succeed': Top Generals Feared Trump Would Attempt a Coup After Election, According to New Book," CNN, July 14, 2021.

28. George Schroeder, "Seminary Presidents Reaffirm BFM, Declare CRT Incompatible," *Baptist Press*, November 30, 2020.

29. Kate Shellnutt, "Southern Baptists Keep Quarreling Over Critical Race Theory," *Christianity Today*, December 3, 2020.

30. Daniel A. Cox, "Rise of Conspiracies Reveals an Evangelical Divide in the GOP," Survey Center on American Life, February 12, 2021.

31. Darragh Roche, "Pat Robertson Faces Backlash After Calling Critical Race Theory 'Monstrous Evil,'" *Newsweek*, June 26, 2021.

32. Tucker Carlson, "Anti-White Mania," *Tucker Carlson Tonight*, June 24, 2021.

33. Sheera Frenkel, "After Capitol, Proud Boys Quietly Shift Focus to Schools and Town Halls," *New York Times*, December 15, 2021.

34. Christopher F. Rufo (@realchrisrufo), Twitter, March 15, 2021, 1:17 p.m., https://twitter.com/realchrisrufo/status/1371541044592996 352?lang=en.

35. Tyler Kinkade, Brandy Zadrozny, and Ben Collins, "Critical Race Theory Battle Invades School Boards—With Help from Conservative Groups," NBC, June 15, 2021; Benjamin Wallace-Wells, "How a Conservative Activist Invented the Conflict Over Critical Race Theory," *The New Yorker*, June 18, 2021.

36. Chris Kahn, "Many Americans Embrace Falsehoods about Critical Race Theory," Reuters, July 15, 2021.

37. Laura Meckler and Josh Dawsey, "Republicans, Spurred by an Unlikely Figure, See Political Promise in Targeting Critical Race Theory," *Washington Post*, June 21, 2021.

38. Executive Order on Combating Race and Sex Stereotyping, September 22, 2020, https://trumpwhitehouse.archives.gov/presi dential-actions/executive-order-combating-race-sex-stereotyping/.

39. Matthew S. Schwartz, "Trump Tells Agencies to End Trainings on 'White Privilege' and 'Critical Race Theory,'" National Public Radio, September 5, 2020.

40. Jenn Selva, "Texas Lieutenant Governor Wants to End Tenure for New University Instructors in Attempt to Stop the Teaching of Critical Race Theory," CNN, February 18, 2022.

41. Rick Perlstein, *Before the Storm: Barry Goldwater and the Unmaking of the American Consensus* (New York: Nation Books, 2009), 228.

42. Schroeder, "Seminary Presidents Reaffirm BFM."

43. "In Changing U.S. Electorate, Race and Education Remain Stark Dividing Lines," Pew Research Center, June 2, 2020.

44. Graham Colton, "Glen Youngkin Vows to Take Bold Stand Against Critical Race Theory as Governor," Fox News, October 31, 2021.

45. I am indebted to one of my dissertation mentors, John Raines, who would constantly remind me of this fact during my doctoral studies.

46. Trip Gabriel and Dana Goldstein, "GOP Challenges Teaching Racism's Scope," *New York Times*, June 2, 2021.

47. Joy-Ann Reid (@JoyAnnReid), Twitter, June 11, 2021, 3:57 p.m., https://twitter.com/JoyAnnReid/status/1403471521876779011?s=20.

48. Alexis de Tocqueville, *Democracy in America*, trans. Arthur Goldhammer (1835; New York: Literary Classics of the United States, 2004), 517–18.

49. Reince Prebus et al., *Republican Platform 2016* (Cleveland: Republican National Convention, 2016), i.

50. Prebus et al., *Republican Platform*, 41.

51. Devan Cole, "Graham Denies Systemic Racism Exists in US and Says 'America's Not a Racist Country,'" CNN Politics, April 25, 2021.

52. See https://www.blackamericansmaga.org/.

53. Ron DeSantis, Speech Introducing the Stop WOKE Act, Wildwood, Florida, December 15, 2021, https://www.youtube.com/watch?v=kWUgjZrBkNY.

54. Mike Baker and Danielle Ivory, "Public Health Crisis Grows with Distrust and Threats," *New York Times*, October 18, 2021.

55. Erin Woo, "How Covid Misinformation Created a Run on Animal Medicine," *New York Times*, September 28, 2021.

56. Patricia Mazzei, "A Miami School Becomes a Beacon for Anti-Vaxxers," *New York Times*, May 2, 2021.

57. Kristen V. Brown and Justin Sink, "Trump's Comment on Disinfectant Prompts Experts to Warn Against Inhaling Bleach to Kill Coronavirus," *Time*, April 24, 2020.

58. Jeffrey Kluger, "Accidental Poisonings Increased After President Trump's Disinfectant Comments," *Time*, May 12, 2020.

59. Jason Wilson, "The Rightwing Christian Preachers in Deep Denial Over Covid-19's Danger," *The Guardian*, April 4, 2020.

60. Bill Hutchinson, "Pastor Says He Won't Close Church after COVID-19 Outbreak Infected 74 Members," ABC News, May 9, 2021.

61. Jennifer Lee, "Kenneth Copeland Wants Private Jet to Avoid Vaccine Mandate," *Christianity Today*, September 25, 2022.

62. "10 Facts about Americans and Coronavirus Vaccines," Pew Research Center, March 22, 2021, https://www.pewresearch.org/fact-tank/2021/09/20/10-facts-about-americans-and-coronavirus-vaccines/ft_21-03-18_vaccinefacts/.

63. Deidre McPhillips, "Unvaccinated People Face 20 Times Greater Risk of Dying from Covid-19 Than Those Who Have Been Boosted, According to US Data," CNN, December 20, 2021.

64. David Leonhardt, "Covid Politics Are Walloping Red America," *New York Times*, September 28, 2021.

65. @NoSpinNews, https://twitter.com/NoSpinNews/status/14729 34353583984641.

66. Cheryl Clark, "Medical Examiners Report Demands to Remove COVID from Death Certificates," Medpage Today, December 16, 2021.

Chapter 5

1. Bob Smietana, "Jericho March Plans DC Return in the New Year to Pray Pence Will Overturn Election," Religion News Service, December 31, 2020.

2. See Robert P. Jones, "Taking the White Christian Nationalist Symbols at the Capitol Riot Seriously," Religion News Service, January 7, 2021.

3. Elaine Godfrey, "It Was Supposed to Be So Much Worse," *The Atlantic*, January 9, 2021.

4. Peter Baker, Maggie Haberman, and Annie Karni, "Pence Reached His Limit with Trump. It Wasn't Pretty," *New York Times*, January 12, 2021.

5. Shira Feder, "Storming of the Capitol Through the Lens of a Veteran Jewish DC Photographer," *The Times of Israel*, January 14, 2021.

6. Adam Goldman, "U.S. Needs More Resources to Fight Rising Threat of Domestic Terror, Report Warns," *New York Times*, March 18, 2021.

7. Jonathan Weisman and Reid J. Epstein, "G.O.P. Calls Riot 'Legitimate Political Discourse,'" *New York Times*, February 5, 2022.

8. Mike Gonzalez, "For Five Months, BLM Protestors Trashed America's Cities. After the Election, Things May Only Get Worse," The Heritage Foundation, November 6, 2020.

9. Roudabeh Kishi and Sam Jones, *Demonstrations & Political Violence in America: New Data for Summer 2020* (Madison, WI: US Crisis Monitor, 2020), 3.

10. Julie Watson, "Comparison Between Capitol Siege, BLM Protests Is Denounced," Associated Press, January 14, 2021.

11. Jonathan Allen, "After Nevada Ranch Stand-Off, Emboldened Militias Ask: Where Next?," Reuters, April 17, 2014.

12. Isaac Arnsdorf, "Oath Keepers in the State House: How a Militia Movement Took Root in the Republican Mainstream," ProPublica, October 20, 2021.

13. Michael S. Schmidt and Luke Broadwater, "Officers' Injuries, Including Concussions, Show Scope of Violence at Capitol Riot," *New York Times*, February 11, 2021.

14. Dan Barry, Alan Feuer, and Matthew Rosenberg, "90 Seconds of Rage on the Capitol Steps," *New York Times*, October 17, 2021.

15. Peter Baker and Sabrina Tavernise, "One Legacy of Impeachment: The Most Complete Account So Far of Jan. 6," *New York Times*, February 13, 2021.

16. Brittany Shammas, "A GOP Congressman Compared Capitol Rioters to Tourists. Photos Show Him Barricading a Door," *Washington Post*, May 18, 2021.

17. Weisman and Epstein, "G.O.P. Calls Riot 'Legitimate Political Discourse.'"

18. Donnie O'Sullivan, "Flynn Says He Didn't Endorse Myanmar-Style Coup After He Appears to Back Plan in Video Exchange," CNN, June 1, 2021.

19. Maggie Haberman and Zolan Kanno-Youngs, "Trump Weighed Naming Election Conspiracy Theorist as Special Counsel," *New York Times*, December 19, 2020.

20. Matt Flegenheimer, "Biden Says Trump Is 'Not Who We Are.' Do Voters Agree?," *The New York Times*, November 3, 2020.

21. David D. Kirkpatrick and Alan Feuer, "Proud Boys Got Bigger as Police Looked Away," *New York Times*, March 15, 2021.

22. James Q. Whitman, *Hitler's American Model: The United States and the Making of Nazi Race Laws* (Princeton: Princeton University Press, 2017), 84, 139.

23. Whitman, *Hitler's American Model*, 35, 38, 40, 51, 93.

24. Scott Neuman, "During Roundtable, Trump Calls Some Unauthorized Immigrants 'Animals,'" National Public Radio, May 17, 2018; Michelle Ye Hee Lee, "Donald Trump's False Comments Connecting Mexican Immigrants and Crime," *Washington Post*, July 8, 2015.

25. A certain arrogance exists for one nation to take the name of an entire hemisphere—"America"—which comprises some thirty-five nations, to be used exclusively for its citizens. Because I was born in Cuba, I am an American because Cuba, by definition, is located within the Americas. Hence, as I write this book, I am experiencing a certain degree of cognitive dissonance every time I refer to US citizens as Americans as if the term was exclusively for them. For this reason, I have insisted on the usage of the term *Euroamerican*.

26. Alex Rogers, "Liz Cheney Loses House Republican Leadership Post Over Feud with Trump," CNN, May 12, 2021.

27. Marie Fazio, "Mitt Romney Is Booed by Members of His Own Party," *New York Times*, May 2, 2021.

28. Alexandra Alter and Elizabeth A. Harris, "Dr. Seuss Books Are Pulled, and a 'Cancel Culture' Controversy Erupts," *New York Times*, March 4, 2021.

29. Joseph Pisani, "Mr. Potato Head Drops the Mister, Sort Of," Associated Press, February 25, 2021.

30. Steve Rose, "Cotton Plantations and Non-consensual Kisses: How Disney Became Embroiled in the Culture Wars," *The Guardian*, May 6, 2021.

31. Eli Rosenberg, "GOP Candidate Blames Human Trafficking on Sexual Liberation, Saying It Leads to 'Slavery' of Women," *Washington Post*, January 31, 2018.

32. Josh Hawley, "Senator Hawley Delivers National Conservatism Keynote on the Left's Attack on Men in America," https://www.hawley .senate.gov/senator-hawley-delivers-national-conservatism-keynote -lefts-attack-men-america.

33. @RightWingWatch, October 18, 2021, 8:53 a.m., https://twit ter.com/i/status/1450097787908022278.

34. Kevin Liptak, "Trump Has Repeatedly Questioned Why Americans Who Served in Vietnam Went to War," CNN, September 5, 2020.

35. "Interview with Donald Trump," *The Howard Stern Show*, May 7, 1998: 7:16. https://www.trumponstern.com/episode/auto-draft-34/#.

36. "In Changing U.S. Electorate, Race and Education Remain Stark Dividing Lines," Pew Research Center, June 2, 2020.

37. Lisa Lerer and Astead W. Herndon, "Menace Enters the Republican Mainstream," *New York Times*, November 12, 2021.

38. John Kruzel, "White Men Have Committed More Mass Shooting Than Any Other Group," *Newsweek*, October 2, 2017.

39. Jonathan Allen, "A 'Duty' to Chase Ahmaud Arbery? Jury in Murder Trial Hears Clashing Accounts," Reuters, November 22, 2021.

40. Erica Chenoweth and Jeremy Pressman, "This Summer's Black Lives Matter Protests Were Overwhelmingly Peaceful, Our Research Finds," *Washington Post*, October 16, 2020.

41. Reid J. Epstein and Patricia Mazzei, "Republicans Sharpen Penalties for Protestors in Flurry of Bills," *New York Times*, April 22, 2021.

42. Catherine Boyle, "Secret to Romney's Defeat: Not Enough 'Angry White Guys'?," CNBC, November 7, 2012.

43. Michel Foucault, preface to *Anti-Oedipus: Capitalism and Schizophrenia*, by Felix Guattari and Gilles Deleuze (New York: Penguin Classics, 2009), xli.

44. Nicholas Riccardi and Anthony Izaguirre, "Conservative Group Boasts of Secret Role in Voting Laws," *Associated Press*, May 14, 2021.

45. Adam Serwer, "Chief Justice Roberts Frames Congress for Voting Rights Act Demise," MSNBC, June 25, 2013.

46. Adam Liptak, "Justices Void Oversight of States, Issue at Heart of Voting Rights Act," *New York Times*, June 26, 2013.

47. Adam Liptak, "Court Is 'One of Most Activist,' Ginsburg Says, Vowing to Stay," *New York Times*, August 24, 2013.

48. "Voting Laws Roundup: December 2021," Brennan Center for Justice, December 21, 2021, https://www.brennancenter.org/our-work /research-reports/voting-laws-roundup-december-2021.

49. Pippa Norris, Ferran Martínez Coma, Alessandro Nai, and Max Grömping, *Why Elections Fail and What We Can Do About It: The Year in Elections, Mid-2016 Update* (Sydney, AU: The Electoral Integrity Project, Department of Government and International Relations, 2016), 5.

50. Scott Bauer, "Trump Adviser: Expect More Aggressive Poll Watching in 2020," Associated Press, December 20, 2019.

51. Donald J. Trump (@realDonaldTrump), November 7, 2012: https://twitter.com/realDonaldTrump/status/266038556504494082 ?ref_src=twsrc%5Etfw (account has been suspended and the original tweet is no longer available).

52. Lorraine C. Minnite, *The Myth of Voter Fraud* (Ithaca: Cornell University Press, 2010), 13.

53. "Presidential Results," CNN Politics, http://www.cnn.com /election/results/president.

54. Michael S. Shear and Maggie Haberman, "Trump Claims, With No Evidence, that 'Millions of People' Voted Illegally," *New York Times*, November 27, 2016.

55. Michael McDonald, "2016 November General Election Turn-

out Rates," United States Election Projects, http://www.electproject .org/2016g.

56. Michael Wines, "All This Talk of Voter Fraud? Across U.S., Officials Found Next to None," *The New York Times*, December 18, 2016.

57. Michael Tackett and Michael Wines, "Trump Disbands Commission on Voter Fraud," *New York Times*, January 3, 2018.

58. Nick Corasaniti and Reid J. Epstein, "Map by Map, G.O.P Erasing Black Districts," *New York Times*, December 18, 2021.

59. Michael Wines, "G.O.P. Gerrymanderer and His Broad Reach," *New York Times*, September 11, 2019.

60. *Rucho et al. v. Common Cause et al.*

61. Reid J. Epstein and Nick Corasaniti, "Jagged Maps Tilt Key Races Toward G.O.P." *New York Times*, November 15, 2021.

62. Reid J. Epstein and Nick Corasaniti, "New Voting Maps Erase Competitive House Seats," *New York Times*, February 7, 2022.

63. Zoltan Hajnal, Nazita Lajevardi, and Lindsay Neilson, "Voter Identification and the Suppression of Minority Votes," *Journal of Politics* 79, no. 2 (2017): 363–64, 372–73.

64. Hajnal et al., "Voter Identification," 366.

65. The Associated Press, "New Rules in these States Are Frustrating Voters," *Fortune*, November 7, 2016.

66. Andy Sullivan and Grant Smith, "Use It or Lose It: Occasional Ohio Voters May Be Shut Out in November," Reuters, June 2, 2016.

67. Sam Levine, "Voter Purges: Are Republicans Trying to Rig the 2020 Election?," *The Guardian*, December 31, 2019.

68. Erin McCormick, Spenser Mestel, and Sam Levine, "Revealed: Wisconsin's Black and Student Populations at Highest Risk of Voter Purge," *The Guardian*, April 6, 2020.

69. Christopher Uggen, Ryan Larson, Sarah Shannon, and Arleth Pulido-Nava, *Locked Out 2020: Estimates of People Denied Voting Rights Due to a Felony Conviction* (Washington, DC: The Sentencing Project, 2020), 4.

70. Uggen et al., *Locked Out 2020*, 4.

71. Ed Pilkington, "In 1981 a 'Task Force' Intimidated Voters at the Polls. Will Republicans Revert to Their Old Tactics?," *The Guardian*, August 24, 2020.

72. Nick Corasaniti, "Republicans Aim to Expand Power of Poll Watchers," *New York Times*, May 2, 2021.

73. Dara Kam, "Former Florida GOP Leaders Say Voter Suppression Was Reason They Pushed New Election Law," *The Palm Beach Post*, November 26, 2012.

74. Adam Brewster and Caitlin Huey-Burns, "What Georgia's New Voting Law Really Does—9 Facts," CBS News, April 7, 2021.

75. Michael Wines, "Republicans Mount Attack on Mail-In Voting Rules," *New York Times*, December 11, 2020.

76. Aaron Black, "Trump Just Comes Out and Says It: The GOP Is Hurt When It's Easier to Vote," *Washington Post*, March 30, 2020.

77. Angelica Stabile, "Gaetz Warns Republicans Will Never Win 'Another National Election Again' If Mail-in Balloting Persists," Fox News, November 30, 2020.

78. Jacob Bogage, "Trump Says Postal Service Needs Money for Mail-in Voting, but He'll Keep Blocking Funding," *Washington Post*, August 12, 2020.

79. Nick Corasaniti, "Rejected Mail Ballots in Texas Disproportionately Affect Black People," *New York Times*, March 19, 2022.

80. Jennifer Medina, Nick Corasaniti, and Reid J. Epstein, "Election Deniers Seek State Posts to Certify Votes," *New York Times*, January 31, 2022.

Chapter 6

1. Miguel A. De La Torre, *Decolonizing Christianity: Becoming Badass Believers* (Grand Rapids: Eerdmans, 2021), 47.

2. Chris Cillizza, "'Let's Go Brandon,' Explained," CNN, November 1, 2021.

3. Paul LeBlanc, "Republican Congressman Details Threatening Voicemail He Received After Voting for Bipartisan Infrastructure Bill," CNN, November 8, 2021.

4. Rebecca Shabad, "Donald Trump Names Favorite Bible Verse," CBS News, April 14, 2016.

5. Donald Trump Jr., "Speech Given at Turning Point USA," December 19, 2021: https://youtu.be/bJ7VDJdFmQU.

6. Donald Trump, "Speech to Family Leadership Summit," *Road to the White House – C-Span*, July 18, 2015: https://www.youtube.com/watch?v=jKRTuT-NHLk.

7. Tim Arango and Giulia Heyward, "Despite Protests, Number of Fatal Police Encounters Is Unchanged," *New York Times*, December 25, 2021.

8. Jason Wilson, "Proud Boys and Other Far-Right Groups Raise Millions Via Christian Funding Site," *The Guardian*, April 10, 2021; Wilson, "US Police and Public Officials Donate to Kyle Rittenhouse, Data Breach Reveals," *The Guardian*, April 16, 2021.

9. Anti-Defamation League Website: https://www.adl.org/white-supremacist-propaganda-spikes-2020.

10. Morgan Gstalter, "Franklin Graham: 'I Think God Was Behind the Last Election,'" The Hill, June 14, 2019.

11. Jeremy Diamond and Kirsten Appleton, "Paula White: Trump's Televangelist in the White House," CNN, November 8, 2019.

12. Ryan Burge, "How Many Americans Believe Trump Is Anointed by God?," Religion News Service, November 25, 2019.

13. "Risk for COVID-19 Infection, Hospitalization, and Death by Race/Ethnicity," Centers for Disease Control and Prevention, November 22, 2021.

14. Pierre Thomas, Yun Choi, Jasmine Brown, and Pete Madden, "Driving while Black: ABC News Analysis of Traffic Stops Reveals Racial Disparities in Several Cities," ABC News, September 9, 2020.

15. Julie Bosman, Sophia Kasakove, and Daniel Victor, "U.S. Life

Expectancy Plunged in 2020, Especially for Black and Hispanic Americans," *New York Times*, July 21, 2021.

16. Astead W. Herndon, "As President Preaches Unity, Charlottesville Calls for Justice," *New York Times*, January 22, 2021.

17. Frederick John Dalton, *The Moral Vision of César Chávez* (Maryknoll: Orbis Books, 2003), 120.

18. Joseph Fletcher, *Situation Ethics: The New Morality* (Louisville: Westminster John Knox, 1966), 69.

19. Matthew Sheffield, "Poll: Most Republicans Think White People Face Discrimination, Democrats Disagree," The Hill, March 8, 2019.